APPLYING LESSONS FROM THE PROTOTYPE

Tony Koester

Kalmbach
Media

Acknowledgements

I extend my sincere appreciation to those who provided information and photos including Gerry Albers, Joe Atkinson, Eric Brooman, Jack Burgess, Kevin Burkholder, Mike Clements, Mike Confalone, Chuck Conway, Bill Darnaby, Mike DelVecchio, Richard Deuso, Larry DeYoung, Andrew Dodge, Paul Dolkos, Jim Dufour, Jared Harper, Frank Hodina, Dave Ingles, Philip Keppers, Tom Klimoski, Jason Klocke, Randy Laframboise, Chris Lantz, Ron Marquardt, Allen McClelland, James McNab, Northern Pacific Ry. Historical Association, Jack Ozanich, Ted Pamperin, Clark Propst, Jim Ramnes, Wayne Sittner, Perry Squier, Paul Swanson of Lake States Archive, Doug Tagsold, Gary Tarbox, Rich Taylor, and Craig Wilson. Special thanks are extended to Jeff Wilson and Diane Bacha, who guided this book through Kalmbach's meticulous production process.

Tony Koester
Newton, N.J.
April 2020

On the cover:

The Nickel Plate Road's first PA-1 accelerates eastbound from a station stop with train No. 10 at Cayuga, Ind., on its way to Cleveland on Oct. 9, 1954. The scene is on Tony Koester's HO model railroad. *Tony Koester photo*

All photos by Tony Koester except where otherwise noted.

Kalmbach Media
21027 Crossroads Circle
Waukesha, Wisconsin 53186
www.KalmbachHobbyStore.com

Published in 2020
24 23 22 21 20   1 2 3 4 5

Manufactured in China

ISBN: 978-1-62700-796-2
EISBN: 978-1-62700-797-9

Editor: Jeff Wilson
Book Design: Kelly Katlaps

Library of Congress Control Number: 2019956990

Contents

Modeling a long-gone railroad such as West Virginia's Buffalo Creek & Gauley is a way to apply lessons from the prototype to preserve railroad and local history, as Brooks Stover has done in S scale (1:64). His most recent effort is a downsized version of his original layout, as he explained in *Model Railroad Planning 2019*. The structures and the bridges in this scene of Dundon, W.Va., where the BC&G interchanged with the Baltimore & Ohio, were built from photos. BC&G 2-8-0 No. 13 is from S Helper Service (later MTH; no longer in business) and is detailed to match the prototype. Brooks built the caboose from a Lake Junction Models kit; the Mack railbus is scratchbuilt. *Brooks Stover*

Something old into something new

What started out as a simple compilation of previously published Trains of Thought commentaries, which have appeared monthly (with two exceptions) in *Model Railroader* since November 1985, expanded into what you have in your hands. I took the more interesting one-page commentaries that related to lessons about how we can apply ways the full-size railroads go about their toil to model railroad planning, construction, and operations and expanded them into chapters on the same topic.

Reinventing the wheel

One thing that model railroaders tend to excel at is reinventing the wheel. Rather than doing even a modicum of homework about prototype practices, we concoct our own ways of doing things.

There may be some degree of satisfaction in having solved problems our own way, but we are, after all, modeling railroading. We're not modeling in a vacuum; we do have benchmarks to reach. Abundant examples have been set for us.

That said, some latitude is not only allowed but also almost mandatory. We don't have gymnasiums in which to locate our miniature railroads, so our first compromise will be a degree of judiciously applied selective compression.

Time and financial budgets will immediately enter the picture.

But by looking to the prototype for information and inspiration, we can save ourselves a lot of missteps. The professionals have figured out how to make railroading work. All we have to do is to work out practical ways to scale that down.

Let's begin that process in Chapter 1 by looking at practical ways to model prototype railroading, whether you're modeling a specific railroad, as Brooks Stover has done (at left, in S scale on his Buffalo Creek & Gauley), or you have selected one or more similar prototypes on which to base a plausible freelanced railroad.

CHAPTER ONE

Pragmatic prototype modeling

If you're modeling alone and only your immediate family will see what you're doing, is there any harm in combining a 21st century locomotive with mid-20th century rolling stock? After all, it's your railroad. Be aware that such arguments wear thin in a surprisingly short time, especially for those espousing to model railroading as it actually exists or existed. Seeing scenes representative of an actual time and place come back to life through accurate modeling is an extremely rewarding endeavor.

A friend is embarking on building a layout. Like many of us, he has a favorite prototype—by coincidence, part of the same division of the railroad I'm modeling—and he wants the railroad to reflect its main attributes. Eager as he is to get started, he—again, like many of us—has some concerns: "I'm stuck between wanting to be as prototypical as possible, yet impatient to get a layout built and running ASAP."

Who's the judge?

He went on to say that as a beginner, he knew that he didn't have the experience that many modelers have, so trying to scratchbuild the downtown area of his hometown as it appeared in the 1950s seemed pretty daunting.

The only people who are likely to see his layout are his wife and kids, and they aren't going to know the difference between Norfolk Southern's "Nickel Plate" ES44AC 8100 pulling a string of 40-foot wood reefers, **1**, or an NKP GP7 pulling double-stacks.

He concluded that he wants to be as realistic as possible for his own sake, but he's willing to bend the visual effects for the sake of simplicity. Maybe.

Another good friend, Ray Breyer, who edits the Nickel Plate Road Historical & Technical Society's free online Modeler's Notebook (check nkphts.org), offered him some advice that is worth sharing:

"If you want to be a 'proto-sincere' modeler," Ray suggested, "there are a few things to keep in mind:

Modeling a specific time and place—here Metcalf, Ill., circa 1954—does not require that everything be a perfect replica. As long as it looks the part, that's often good enough. The depot was scratchbuilt by Randy Laframboise, but the elevator is a stock Walthers kit, and the grain bins are Resin Car Works castings.

• Do as much research as practical, and don't be afraid to ask questions.

• Keep in mind that knowing what reality looks like and what a model 'needs' to look like are actually two different things.

• Stick firmly with your goal, which should be modeling a single year, or even a single month. Fewer distractions and alternatives mean faster progress!

• Realize that you'll never know everything about your goal, and don't let that be a hindrance to your progress.

• Don't be afraid to do something one year and go back and fix mistakes a few years down the road.

• Be a pragmatic modeler. Be as accurate as your time, finances, skills, knowledge, and artistic vision allow.

• Finally, keep in mind that you can never actually model each and every rivet, and that you don't actually need to, especially once the trains start rolling.

"Look to those who are better modelers than you are for inspiration, guidance, and advice," Ray added. "But never fall into the trap of thinking that, just because you're not as good as they are, you might as well give up and do nothing."

His conclusion was equally on the mark: "Keep firmly in mind that building a model railroad isn't a contest. Nobody's judging you, this isn't life or death, and it's supposed to be fun. I fell into the trap of trying to model my pet prototype 'perfectly.' I ended up with modeling paralysis for a decade, simply because I couldn't fit exactly what I wanted into my layout space. I finally wised up, scaled back, and became a proto-freelancer. Nine months later, I am almost done laying track. And I'm much happier!"

Ray added a footnote: "If the rivet counters give you grief, just remind them that some of the hobby's most respected modelers are freelancers!"

Knowing it "all"

I want to spend a little time on Ray's fourth bullet point: "Realize that you'll never know everything about your goal, and don't let that be a hindrance

to your progress."

I have seen some really worthwhile modeling projects derailed by a lack of understanding or full acceptance of this statement. You've heard the expression "analysis paralysis," and it's a very real phenomenon. Much of what we need to know will not be revealed to us until we take the first tentative steps toward our goals. We won't learn a lot of what we want to know for a long time after we'd really like to have that information in hand. Some of those initial steps will therefore be missteps, wastes of time and resources, but oh-so-valuable lessons that will pay handsome dividends later on.

While we're waiting for information about a town or a depot to materialize, there is no reason not to build the benchwork and lay the track that will facilitate early operations. Almost every railroad town on the continent has been documented by a railroad-specific historical society and is available online or through an online contact, so waiting for "more information" is no longer a valid excuse. As Ray said, you'll never have "all" of the information you desire, so take your best shot. If better data show up later, great—you now have a new modeling project in the form of an upgrade ahead of you, **2**.

I also started to write that, as one who is doing his best to model a specific prototype, I try to follow that prototype's example to the best of my ability. But that's not true. If I tried to do everything as well as I possibly can, I wouldn't get much done. It's only when one becomes comfortable with a certain degree of compromise—not

too much, not too little—that real progress occurs.

Building a model railroad, especially a basement-size model railroad, is all about compromise. Allen McClelland's famous "Good Enough" principle applies here, **3**. I do things as well as I think is required to convey the impression of that prototype in that time and place. I try to do everything from room preparation to model building to operating procedures to the same level of quality and realism. There's little sense in doing *This* to extreme tolerances while doing *That* to a lesser standard.

The deck girder bridge over the Little Vermilion River near Humrick, Ill., **4**, and the deck truss bridge over the Embarras River west of Oakland, Ill., are good examples of using commercial products that resemble the prototype structures to a sufficient degree and thus saved me considerable time compared to scratchbuilding these key bridges.

The Maple Hotel at Charleston, Ill., **5**, is another example of making do with commercial kit components when information about two of the structure's four walls is lacking and the building plays a minor scenic role. Moreover, the two unknown walls are virtually invisible when the structure is positioned on the railroad. (I can hear Dave Frary telling me I shouldn't have wasted time and materials building them!)

The end result

What I have achieved has proven pleasing, **6**, if not always an exact replica of an actual scene I discovered along the Nickel Plate's Third Sub.

Blending prototype-based modeling with prototype modeling greatly strengthens the plausibility of the latter. Here the Chesapeake & Ohio's *George Washington* **is at Deepwater, W.Va., heading west to Cincinnati in the Kanawha River valley, which provides a convenient thoroughfare for both the C&O and the Virginian & Ohio's K&M Division. On the north bank, V&O No. 12, the** *Mail & Express,* **heads to Afton, Va. Everything Allen McClelland did on both HO versions of the Virginian & Ohio and continues to do today on the segment of the V&O that complements Gerry Albers' Virginian layout, as shown here, was built to the same level of quality, one that Allen deemed "good enough." This principle—covering everything from scenery to detailing to paperwork—is now applied with considerable success by many modelers, including me, to their own work.** *Gerry Albers*

4

5

To me, it is indeed Good Enough. I've gotten a lot done in a decade and a half. My crew seems to enjoy running the railroad as my publishing and travel schedule allows time for operating sessions.

So I have high hopes for my neophyte friend finding satisfaction in this hobby, especially if he heeds Ray's advice. It worked for me.

Limiting your options

Constraining one's choices doesn't sound like a particularly desirable course of action, but it actually can be quite helpful. For starters, it can help to avoid that bane of all hobby endeavors: analysis paralysis.

Let's consider the most basic of problems facing railroaders who work in any scale from Z up to full size:

switching cars. I'll pose a switching problem, and then you decide how many yard tracks it will require to solve it.

The eastbound yard at Frankfort, Ind., is as good an example as any. Trains arriving from the west are routinely sorted into blocks: "propers," which are for distribution in Frankfort; "locals," which are cars to be

The key "signature" scene on my HO railroad is the steel deck girder bridge over the Little Vermilion River near the Indiana–Illinois state line (left). It was easily kitbashed using Micro Engineering piers and towers plus Central Valley girders to approximate the appearance of the prototype. The deck-truss bridge over the Embarras ("AHM-braw") River west of Oakland, Ill. (above), was kitbashed from a Central Valley through truss bridge kit built by Jim Kelly, thus achieving a prototypical appearance while saving considerable time compared to scratchbuilding.

The Maple Hotel adjacent to the NKP depot at Charleston, Ill., was kitbashed using Design Preservation Models no. 243-10300 (Cutting's Scissor Co.) kits based on a single photo (left) and information from a Sanborn fire insurance map. Fortunately, the two unseen walls are also unseen when the structure is positioned on the layout (above). The key to kitbashing such structures is to study potential kits, watching for window details such as width and height, number of panes, and lintel and similar details. Hard-to-disguise joints between brick wall sections can often be concealed behind downspouts, electrical conduits, plumbing lines, vines, or nearby power poles or trees. *Prototype photo: Jacob Hortenstine collection*

distributed to towns between Frankfort and the next division point yard east of there; and "throughs," which are destined to or beyond the next division point.

Making the job a bit more complicated is the fact that there are four divisions radiating out of Frankfort: two to the east and two to the west. We'll consider only the two

to the east: the Toledo and Sandusky divisions.

The cars for Toledo and Sandusky Division local freights have to be blocked in station order to make switching easier and more efficient for the local's crew. There are quite a few towns between Frankfort and the next division points.

Assuming the inbound freights

were properly blocked—propers, Toledos, and Sanduskys—it would be nice if Frankfort's eastbound yardmaster took time to add outbound cars to the proper blocks.

Now then, at an absolute minimum, how many yard tracks does the eastbound yardmaster need?

Just two. You can sort any cut of cars into any required sequence

Some scenes are of necessity generic. When efforts to locate a model-worthy farm scene between Frankfort and Linden, Ind., came to naught, I used commercial kits to create a generic arrangement of farm buildings. I'm still tweaking the scene, which is part of the fun.

Frankfort's eastbound yardmaster has 8 of the prototype's 14 yard tracks to work with on my HO railroad. Is that enough? Frankly, it has to be, as the benchwork here is already pretty wide, and the leads to the westbound yard and Swift soybean plant are on the other side of the main from the eastbound yard. Additional tracks would make working the bean plant more difficult.

using two tracks. But they'd have to be very long tracks. And efficiency (throughput) would plunge.

Ideally, he'd have at least three tracks for propers, Toledos, and Sanduskys. Another two tracks on which to build the Toledo and Sandusky locals would be nice. And a "for-now" track is always handy, as is an arrival and a departure track, plus a caboose track.

But two tracks are sufficient, and you can find many examples of that

situation on small railroads, including many of today's regionals.

Considering the larger picture that comprises all aspects of prototype railroading and ways to model it, this is a simplistic example. But it does make my point: We can consider so many options that our brains develop "dial tone," easy solutions escape our attention, and progress ceases.

Looking back at Frankfort's eastbound yard, the prototype yardmaster had 14 yard tracks to work

with. I have modeled eight of those tracks, **7**. Assuming he's building an outbound on one track and keeping another open for an arriving train, he still has six tracks to work with. Is that enough?

The trains we receive in and send out of that yard are shorter than their prototypes, but this has little effect on blocking. We model every single scheduled freight, quite a few sections thereof, and an extra or two. Obviously, unless the yardmaster

works with the general yardmaster, roundhouse foreman, and the fellow who handles all trains in and out of east-end staging to keep his yard fluid, he's in trouble. But it appears that I managed to provide enough yard tracks. Adding more would have made a wide yard even wider. Maybe I erred a track or two either way, but I made a decision based on physical limitations and moved ahead. We'll manage.

The key to moving ahead is to consider a limited, tightly defined set of options, do a modest amount of due diligence on each, make a choice, and then work hard to convert that choice into a very good choice. The alternative is to endlessly weigh your options, which is a sure way not to make headway. You are never going to know everything you think you need to know about anything.

The fine print
If you read the fine print, you'll discover that all of Bill Darnaby's Maumee Route cabooses have the name of the division to which they are assigned "stenciled" on the side, **8**. This reflects the then-standard practice of assigning cabooses not only to specific divisions but also to specific conductors. This made sense, as each crew actually ate and slept in the conductor's assigned caboose when they were overnighting away from their home terminals. One tends to be picky about how his home-away-from-home is decorated and maintained.

Seeing this, I decided to assign cabooses to each of the one modeled and four staged divisions on my depiction of that region of the Nickel Plate. Why, I could even number my cabooses for those that were in service there. And as long as we were being overly ambitious, we could assume the roles of specific conductors who worked those divisions!

Bad idea. It hasn't been easy to find out precisely which cabooses operated out of Frankfort, Ind., and Charleston, Ill., in the 1950s, let alone to whom they were assigned. Thanks to a copy of an engineer's time book given to me by my chief consultant, retired NKP engineer Don Daily, I was able

to determine that my former next-door neighbor, an NKP Third Sub conductor named Griffith, had caboose 1053. A few more names and numbers could be matched up, but doing so for the entire fleet was far too ambitious.

So another overly ambitious idea was filed under "A bridge too far."

How bad do you want it?
Bill once made a rather profound statement that anyone contemplating the construction of a layout, especially a large home layout, needs to take to heart: "If you really want a model railroad, you'll have one." That may sound a little harsh, but Bill's point is that those who have built home layouts made significant commitments of time and money to do so.

There are exceptions to any "rule," of course, but the underlying sentiment here is rock solid. I have made many career and lifestyle decisions based on the unshakable objective of having the space to build a model railroad of the type I wanted.

I'm quite sure I could contact notable layout builders such as Allen McClelland, who built two basement editions of the famous Virginian & Ohio, **3**, and Doug Tagsold, who has built several basement-size home layouts in HO and On3 and now in unique 1:72 proportion, **9**, and I'm confident they would say the same thing: They made life and career decisions that ensured they had the means and locations to build the types of model railroads they wanted.

Is this a "reasonable" attitude? Your mileage may vary, of course. But the time to come to grips with such concerns is at a point between the time when you're impressed with someone else's model railroad of whatever size and scope and your decision to build your own layout. Be sure your commitment and resources are equal to the task.

The locomotive roster
It's one thing to say you're going to model the Cowabunga & Northern in 1923 and quite another to round up the needed motive power to do so. Even if you discover to your delight

Maumee Route cabooses are assigned to specific divisions. This reflects standard prototype practice during and shortly after the steam era when cabooses were assigned to specific conductors and served as their homes away from home when they overnighted at "away" terminals. *Bill Darnaby*

that some now-extinct brass importer brought in 10 models of the C&N's pair of 2-6-0 Camelbacks, you still have a very steep mountain to climb: Can you find two of them? Can you afford them? Do they run well? If not, can you afford to have them rebuilt and perhaps detailed up to today's standards and custom painted, or do you have the time and/or skills to do that yourself? Will they pull 10 hoppers filled with anthracite coal up Cowabunga Mountain?

This is indeed perhaps the best of all times to be a scale model railroader. If you can't afford one of today's DCC

Doug Tagsold has built basement-size railroads in HO, On3, and now 1:72, which represents the Colorado & Southern's narrow-gauge lines using HO locomotive boilers, mechanisms, "old-time" carbodies, and track, but with other details such as locomotive cabs and structures scaled up to the larger proportion. Doug plans all scenery projects so as not to interfere with the following month's operating session. *Doug Tagsold*

sound-equipped superdetailed models, the old DC ones are still sold at swap meets. Some really obscure shortline power is commercially available with factory-applied paint rivaling the best custom work.

But as Andrew Dodge, **6-2**, and Doug Tagsold discovered, not everything will be handed to you on a silver platter. To them, that was a plus; to others, it would be a showstopper. Be sure you understand which side of the fence your choices and desires put you on.

That also applies to some types of rolling stock. Ted Pamperin models the Mann's Creek, a 3-foot-gauge railroad that fed coal and lumber to the Chesapeake & Ohio at Sewell, W.Va., **10**. Red Ball once made a kit for the MC's wood hopper cars but to standard-gauge width, so Ted had to first find enough kits and then narrow their components to fit his HOn3 railroad. Not everyone is going to be up to such a challenge. The alternative would be to use a non-prototypical type of hopper or to model a different railroad.

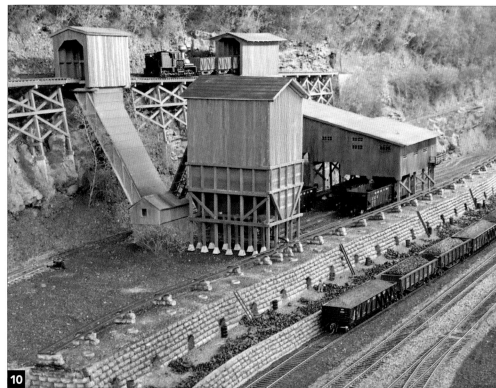

Ted Pamperin models the Mann's Creek narrow-gauge railroad, which fed coal, coke, and lumber products to the Chesapeake & Ohio at Sewell, W.Va. This Shay-powered railroad hauled coal down the mountain in wooden hoppers, which Ted kitbashed by carefully narrowing standard-gauge versions once produced as kits by Red Ball. *Ted Pamperin*

1

CHAPTER TWO

Finding pieces of the puzzle

Designing and building a prototype-based model railroad is much like assembling a puzzle, as each piece is unique and has to interlock with adjacent pieces in a specific order to form a coherent picture. The puzzle pieces are called Layout Design Elements (LDEs), which are visually and operationally recognizable models of actual locations such as towns, yards, engine terminals, harbors, and familiar scenes. *Bill Zuback*

I enjoy solving puzzles of all types. I can't resist a complex picture puzzle, **1**. Bill Darnaby and I and a woman from Australia, who was obviously more experienced at picture-puzzle solving than we were, tackled a monster puzzle while on a 12-day cruise—and beat it! In most cases, the challenges and satisfaction of fitting disparate pieces together into a coherent whole are well worth the time and effort.

During the 1960s and earlier years, it was commonplace to watch local freights switch industries in town while you took photos and chatted with crew members and the station agent about what was going on, thereby learning how the railroad went about earning a living. The crew in the photo at right will have to run around the car they're picking up at Wingate, Ind.; see photo 7.

2

Professional and model railroader Barry Karlberg agrees. "The one thing that will only get better with time," Barry recently said to a group of modelers who regularly chat online, "is the ease of obtaining prototype information faster. The research performed to build a prototype layout is often one of the most rewarding parts of prototype modeling. It's like finding pieces of a puzzle and putting them together.

"With respect to my current project," Barry added, "the research has been the most fun. However, a key source of information is rapidly disappearing for transition-era modelers: railroaders and townspeople, most retired, who worked for the railroads and industries and who performed the jobs we wish to simulate. I would imagine that many of the sources of this information have already passed on or reside in retirement homes."

So we have two topics to ponder: Doing one's homework can be as much or more fun as using that information to build and operate our models. And the sources of first-hand information about how a railroad or related industry worked are perishable.

Let's chat about the last topic first. I recently read a comment by a fellow I've known via correspondence for years. He observed that many, perhaps most, model railroaders don't have a clue how a railroad actually goes about its daily toil. This is understandable for several reasons.

Most obvious is that they may have been drawn to scale model railroading by the innate attractiveness of the models themselves. Many modelers just enjoy building eye-catching or highly detailed models. That they happen to be based on railroad themes is almost incidental.

3

Quite a few of you who are reading this book became interested in model railroading during the era when there was a professional railroader or two in almost every town—a station agent or towerman, perhaps—who was more than happy to chat with you about what he or she did for a living. There was more "loose car" freight (single cars, many to small local industries and businesses) that originated or terminated in small towns, so watching a local (way freight, patrol, etc.) train switch cars was a normal, everyday occurrence, **2**.

Today, it's hard to talk to railroaders without trespassing, and post 9/11 they have to initially assume you're a potential threat to the railroad. The good news is that, as Barry stated, despite such obstacles, it is indeed easier than ever before to do one's due diligence. The real obstacle is acquiring the motivation to look for information—to solve the puzzle.

No matter how many times more experienced modelers tell you how rewarding it is to dig deeply into the art and science of the railroad industry, many of you will roll your eyes and go back to building models that please you rather than those that will support

realistic operation. Some of you will tell me that, frankly, you're getting a little tired of the incessant drumbeat that you interpret to mean you're a lower class of modeler unless you also operate your trains as realistically as they appear.

Perhaps Barry and my puzzle analogy will help you to understand why we routinely mention the rewards of putting your models through their paces based on how full-size railroads actually work. As Barry said, gathering the required background information or then applying that is much like solving a puzzle. Solving puzzles must be popular, as newspapers print a lot of them, and television channels host them as well. Consider the long run of "Jeopardy."

Modeling railroading is therefore akin to solving a series of puzzles. It's not that you're a second-class citizen if you don't operate your railroad realistically. Rather, it's a matter of not realizing the full value of your hard-won modeling efforts. Operating your railroad realistically is like earning a bonus at essentially no additional cost.

You already have the hardware. There's no better time than now to enjoy finding and assembling the

puzzle pieces that will lead you to understand and appreciate how the prototypes for your models earned their keep.

A sterling example

The sign says JOSLIN. It's a good thing it's there, as there's not much else to identify this place in the backcountry of New Hampshire, **3**. Indeed, you could call a great deal of the entire Granite State "rural" without offending anyone. They're rather proud of their home's quaintness and isolation, in fact. These are the good folks who proclaim "Live Free or Die" on their license plates.

So when you describe the Boston & Maine's wood depot in Joslin as marking a wide spot in the road, you're not saying anything exceptional. You're simply describing what makes the state so appealing to so many.

And among the many is Jim Dufour, who models part of the B&M's line that ran from Bellows Falls, Vt., and through Keene, N.H., on its way to the B&M main line in Massachusetts. As Philip R. Hastings' myriad images attest, New Hampshire is about as modelable a state as there is, packed to the borders with

The wood-frame Boston & Maine depot that once marked a spot called Joslin in the timetable isn't very remarkable, which makes it a good modeling candidate. In fact, the relative lack of *anything* remarkable at Joslin makes it a very good modeling candidate. Above: Consolidation 2717 has completed its switching duties along the South Keene spur and is returning to its train with an empty Soo Line grain car. The South Keene spur left the B&M's Cheshire Branch at Joslin to serve a small cluster of nearby industries. *Two photos: Jim Dufour*

Local freight XW-2 has cleared up on the siding at Troy, N.H., to await the passage of a westbound passenger train. Once the westbound has departed, K-8c 2717 will finish switching the sidings at Troy before continuing its eastward journey along the Cheshire Branch as superbly modeled in HO scale by Jim Dufour. *Jim Dufour*

scratchbuilding and Layout Design Element candidates. That's what Jim's HO B&M is—a series of thoughtfully chosen and superbly executed LDE puzzle pieces, which are visually and operationally recognizable models of actual locations, **4**.

Model railroading used to be about intensity. We packed every inch with structures and track. We ran trains on streetcar schedules. But gradually we have come to realize that more isn't necessarily, or even usually, better. Giving each model some breathing room is now seen as a worthy goal, one

5

that runs hand-in-hand with realism. Gerry Leone discussed this in *Model Railroad Planning* 2017 in his article "Spaces between places."

The previous assumption was that action equaled fun. If trains weren't always on the move, we grew bored. And so it remains in some quarters today. But others like Jim are showing us that a static scene like this view of Joslin can be as rewarding to model and view as one that features almost perpetual motion. The payback comes

in the form of re-creating a scene that once was, that we missed by virtue of age or location, one that we can now see in 3-D once again, thanks to thoughtful and diligent modeling.

This is a clear case of the journey being as rewarding as the destination. If Jim knew nothing about the real Joslin of the 1950s and was simply modeling an eye-catching depot, he'd lack a yardstick to measure his success beyond the four walls of the structure. But as he did his due diligence and

came to know Joslin like someone who grew up there, he came to appreciate the little things.

And he came across questions to answer. For example, how did petroleum products like gasoline get from that tank car on the siding across the tracks from the storage tanks? Turns out, Jim discovered, that there was a pipe laid under the tracks. Mystery solved.

There wasn't a lot more to learn about Joslin, at least as far as the

Yosemite Valley authority and modeler Jack Burgess's HO railroad is a museum-quality tribute to the YV that operates as well as it looks, but Jack's true enjoyment comes from the research and craftsmanship required to build the models (also see 5-1). *Jack Burgess*

railroad was concerned. Other than the spur for the tank car, there was a team track that extended beyond the back of the depot to serve a small cluster of industries. Here an occasional car with a load for a local concern, maybe a lumberyard or feed mill, could be spotted for unloading. There's also a passing track here for the occasional meet, orchestrated by a distant dispatcher using timetable and train-order rules. "OS Joslin," the agent-operator would report. "Show

No. 5503 by at 11:32," he'd tell the dispatcher (DS).

A photo backdrop greatly extends the narrow 3-D scenery, proving once again that we used to waste acres of scenery materials to create the scenic depth that a photo does ever so much more convincingly. The viewer isn't prompted to think, "Oh, that scene is only 15" deep." It could be a hundred yards to the woods.

Note that the fascia is painted an unobtrusive green that blends in with

the local flora. The very last thing we're trying to do is to call attention to the picture frame. Ironically, having no frame at all would do just that.

"Model the ordinary"—the white houses, the lonely rural depot, the wide-open spaces—is the new mantra. And Jim is doing an exceptional job of doing just that.

It's all about selecting the proper puzzle pieces, arranging them in the proper order, and giving them room to breathe.

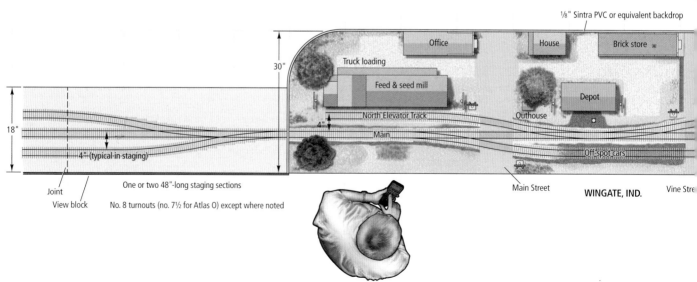

⅛" Sintra PVC or equivalent backdrop

Office

House

Brick store

Truck loading

30"

Feed & seed mill

North Elevator Track

4"

Depot

Outhouse

18"

Main

4" (typical in staging)

Off-spot cars

Joint

One or two 48"-long staging sections

Main Street

WINGATE, IND.

Vine Stre

View block

No. 8 turnouts (no. 7½ for Atlas O) except where noted

6

I added a crossover (just to the right of the hopper car) to the prototype's track arrangement at Wingate, Ind., to allow facing-point pick-ups and setouts to be made without the need for "drops" or the use of a poling pole, which professional crews might have used in the steam era.

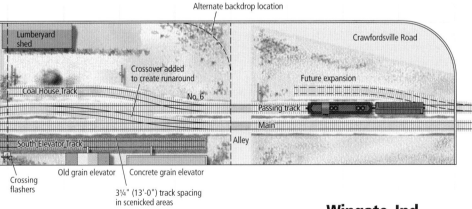

Alternate backdrop location

Lumberyard shed

Crawfordsville Road

Crossover added to create runaround

Coal House Track

No. 6

Future expansion

Passing track

Main

Alley

South Elevator Track

Crossing flashers

Old grain elevator

Concrete grain elevator

3¼" (13'-0") track spacing in scenicked areas

Wingate, Ind.

O scale (1:48)
Size: 30" x 16 feet plus 8-foot extension
Scale of plan: ⅝" = 1'-0", 12" grid
Numbered arrows indicate photo locations
Illustration by Rick Johnson

➕ Find more plans online in the ModelRailroader.com Track Plan Database.

Sanity check

One of the absolute best examples of prototype modeling is Jack Burgess's HO scale Yosemite Valley, **5**, which is set not only in a specific year—1939—but a specific month—August. Jack has scratchbuilt everything on the railroad, sometimes two or even three times, to ensure that it is as close a miniaturization of the actual car or structure that graced this California railroad as his ample skills and knowledge will allow.

But Jack is what I might call a reluctant operator. It's not that he doesn't enjoy operating his railroad as realistically as it appears. Rather, he derives a lot more enjoyment from the craftsmanship required to build the models.

There's no reason to delve into his motivation in this regard. I simply want to point out that this is a legitimate form of prototype modeling. If you find your interests tend more toward model building than operation, look to Jack as your benchmark. But you'll be looking up, as he has set a very high standard of excellence.

What's that track for?

In the first (1995) issue of *Model Railroad Planning,* I introduced the term Layout Design Element. It wasn't a new concept but rather a new way of looking at the piece-parts of model railroad design. Instead of randomly linking a bunch of made-up towns, freelancer and prototype modeler alike would choose actual locations to model as faithfully as space allowed. Layout design was thus reduced primarily to the task of selecting LDEs ("puzzle pieces") and fitting them into the available space.

My goal then, as now, was to teach modelers that it's easier to copy from the prototype and the professionals than to become professional-grade track planners ourselves. Better still, we could proceed with layout design knowing two key things: Each LDE had to work, just as it did for the full-size railroad. And even if we didn't quite fathom exactly how it worked, we could move full-steam ahead, secure in the knowledge that when we did figure it out, that part of the railroad would be ready and waiting for us to use it properly.

There is a caveat, however, as I discussed in the Wingate series of articles in January through April 2020 issues of *Model Railroader:* Professional railroaders could "drop" cars into facing-point sidings, using their momentum to roll them past the locomotive into a "blind" siding. We can't do that, so—as I did with the track arrangement at Wingate, Ind., **6**—sometimes a crossover may need to be added to facilitate a runaround move to position the locomotive behind a car or cut of cars.

The essence of layout design using LDEs was distilled in my book, *Realistic Model Railroad Building Blocks* (Kalmbach, 2005), so I won't dwell on that here. But I will provide a good example as to why I remain so bullish on this methodology.

I lived in the small west-central Hoosier town of Cayuga during the last four years of steam and first four years of dieselization on the Nickel Plate Road's St. Louis line. I spent a lot of time down by the depot and interlocking tower that marked the NKP's crossing of the Chicago & Eastern Illinois' Evansville-Chicago double-track main (**7-6**). I was still a teenager when we moved north to Long Beach, Ind., on Lake Michigan, but I thought I had a pretty good handle on what the NKP did for a living, especially in Cayuga.

When I decided to switch from prototype-based freelancing to prototype modeling, picking the Nickel Plate was a no-brainer. USRA light Mikados, Berkshires, and Alco PAs are a hard combination to top! But I was even more fortunate to have grown up on this part of the NKP than I initially realized, as it was a single-track railroad employing a timetable and train-order dispatching system. This puts most of the decision-making about whether a train can safely move in the hands of its crew rather than the dispatcher, which tends to keep everyone's head in the game.

On this occasion, however, let's focus on the LDE concept's benefits. I'm not always rigorous about taking my own counsel, but on this occasion I did. My HO edition of the Third Sub is nothing more than a series of town and scenic LDEs arranged in the proper geographical order. However, had it not been for Bill Darnaby's coaching about the benefits of a multi-deck railroad that accommodated two crew-change terminals and Frank Hodina's insightful way of wringing the most out of the available space—and a bit more I hadn't even considered—I would have been able to model only half as many LDEs.

One LDE was naturally my former hometown, Cayuga. This was a given but also a good choice because a water tower was located here near the midpoint of the run between Frankfort, Ind., and Charleston, Ill. Frank and I managed to include virtually all of the NKP's track here as well as the interchange and diamond crossings with the C&EI.

We didn't give much thought to the NKP track in Cayuga. We didn't have to, as I had the official NKP track diagram book that showed every track and gave its name, which usually revealed its function. The track serving the brickyard west of town that my dad managed was labeled "Brick Track," for example.

But there was a pair of tracks that left me a little puzzled: the North Track just north of the main, and the Storage Track south of it. There was also a Passing Track, **7**, so what were the other two used for?

Only when regular operating sessions began and we discovered that train No. 45, the westbound KC Local, couldn't haul all the empties needed by online industries did it dawn on us what those tracks were for. Empties, especially 40-foot boxcars for grain loading, could be stored at the midpoint of the railroad for distribution by the local.

As I had postulated when defining the Layout Design Element concept, the railroad knew what it needed. All I had to do was copy it and then await the day when I finally figured it all out.

The arrangement of tracks at Cayuga, Ind., included the main line, a passing track south of the main (where the local is working), a North Track (holding the cut of cars to the left of the local), a South Track (just right of the engine), a Storage Track (holding cars in the distance), and a track serving the Standard Oil dealer. I modeled them all, which was a good thing, as we later discovered Cayuga was where empty boxcars were stored for the westbound (and only) local to "reload" for its trek over the second half of the subdivision.

7

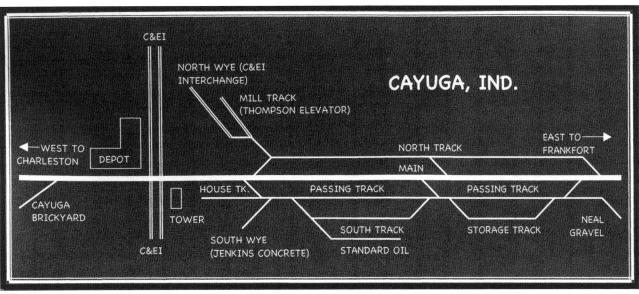

CAYUGA, IND.

C&EI

NORTH WYE (C&EI
INTERCHANGE)

MILL TRACK
(THOMPSON ELEVATOR)

EAST TO
FRANKFORT

WEST TO
CHARLESTON

DEPOT

NORTH TRACK

MAIN

HOUSE TK.

PASSING TRACK

PASSING TRACK

CAYUGA
BRICKYARD

TOWER

SOUTH TRACK

STORAGE TRACK

NEAL
GRAVEL

C&EI

SOUTH WYE
(JENKINS CONCRETE)

STANDARD OIL

CHAPTER THREE

When 'to scale' is too big

The use of smaller-scale models in the background can suggest to the viewer that they are farther away than they actually are and hence that the scene is actually much deeper than it really is. This photo on Paul Dolkos' former Boston & Maine HO layout shows HO trees and fencing in the foreground and an N scale barn and farmhouse in the background. "I think that worked because there was a 'tapered' barbed wire fence and road leading up to the barn and house," Paul commented. "You've got to do more than just drop some smaller-scale structures in the background." *Paul Dolkos*

We profess to be scale model railroaders. But there are occasions when the word "scale" can be a burden in our quest to model the prototype. We embraced the term "selective compression" to cover those times when we need to judiciously reduce the size of our models in ways we hope will not compromise their visual impact, authenticity, and plausibility. And sometimes it's not compromising on scale size but rather in the careful use of perspective that saves the day—for example, the use of N scale models in the background of an HO scene, **1**, to suggest they are farther away than they actually are.

Here's the scene looking north up Division Street in Cayuga, Ind. (above). Below left is how Hutchins' Café looked in the 1990s, and below right is how the scene would have appeared with a scale-size "flat." Using just a photo backdrop greatly improved the perspective in the final scene; the café no longer dominates the scene.

2

When smaller is better

A good example of how reducing the size of a model, or in this case a photo of a structure, to less than actual scale proportions can be helpful is Hutchins Café in Cayuga, Ind.

I have a lot of history in that café. For example, as a kid learning the ropes in the 1950s, I discovered how to balance a pinball machine on my toes to lessen the slope of the table, thus giving me more time to rack up points and win free games, which I then played honestly with the machine back on the floor. Mrs. Hutchins also made sugar-cream pies that are still my idea of the best food in the universe. I have yet to coax her recipe out of the tightly clutched fist of daughter Kay.

I was waiting tables there after school when a loud crash and the sound of breaking glass caused everyone to rush to the front door. There was a bar across the street, and someone had tossed someone else through the front plate-glass window. The town's deputy constable, a frail old man who weighed maybe 90 pounds soaking wet, ambled over to the ensuing fistfight and told them to "Stop right now or I'll call the police!" All of us kids laughed at that, which embarrassed and aggravated old Lou, the man with the badge if not the backbone.

As you might imagine, I had great plans for modeling that café. I had photographed it in 1971 when Jon Marx, Bob Walker, and I drove along the Indiana half of the Nickel Plate Road's Third Subdivision to gather information. But I lacked a

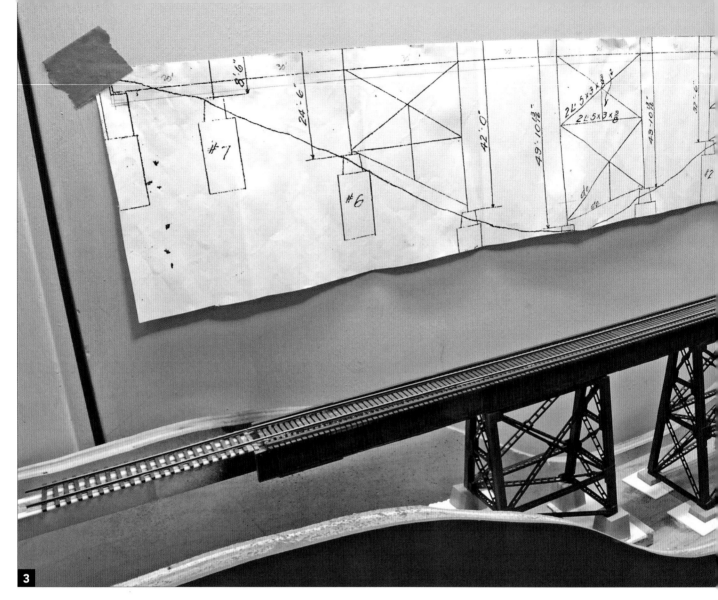

3

good, perfectly lit side view, so in the late 1990s I went back to my 1950s hometown and shot it again.

By then, it had segued into a Mexican restaurant with the lower half of the south side, facing the tracks, now featuring a brightly painted mural, **2**. Photoshop Elements was invented to make such distractions disappear, however, and I quickly cloned upper-story bricks to fill in for those that had been painted over. I also erased the fire escape, figuring that adding this in 3-D would make the building flat more convincing.

I then made a scale-size color print, which I planned to mount to a thick piece of styrene or Sintra, a versatile ABS material used by sign painters that has myriad modeling applications that I learned about from City Classics' Jim Sacco.

Print in hand, I headed back

down to the railroad to see how it would look when positioned against a photo backdrop that looks north up Division Sreet. It looked, well, kinda big, as you can see for yourself in the accompanying photo.

Moreover, there was no front, yet perspective demanded that the front of the building be visible with its top and bottom angling off to a vanishing point down the street. Worse, the scale print seemed to diminish the already compressed space between the café and the NKP interchange track with the Chicago & Eastern Illinois. A curved ramp was supposed to be in that space to allow trucks to climb up into an elevated grain dumping area in Thompson's grain elevator.

Fortunately, the original retouched image from which I had made the scale-size south-wall print had already been glued to the wall. I simply

4

planned to cover it up with the new print. When I removed the scale-size print and looked down the street at eye level, it was abundantly clear that my clever idea of adding some relief to this structure was not such a good idea after all. The photo backdrop alone was a much better solution to the need to populate Division Street with structures.

My entire layout is ringed with a continuous photo backdrop. Most of it is a series of stock or slightly kitbashed "kits" from SceniKing (sceniking. com). But where I have been able to shoot photos of actual locations on the former NKP and successfully backdate them to the 1950s by removing modern vehicles and signage, I have employed these images instead.

The idea of modeling Hutchins' Café in full scale, however, was just too appealing for me to ignore. Fortunately, I caught the error of my ways in time to avoid gluing the ersatz bas-relief version to the wall. Thank goodness I hadn't invested time and materials into building a "flat" of the structure; that would have been even harder to discard.

Memorable bridge scenes

You might think that a flatlands railroad like the Nickel Plate wouldn't have much to offer the bridge-building modeler, but there are four memorable steel bridge scenes on my railroad. Only one of them, **3**, was built to match a prototype drawing and is full scale in both height and length. The others involve compromises that, in my opinion, do not diminish their visual impact.

I devoted a full 8 feet to the

Left: I built the deck-girder bridge over Coal Creek not far east of the NKP's Wabash River crossing using a prototype drawing to its full-scale height and length. By good fortune, it neatly fits on a lift-out section that spans the 36" door opening into the garage.

Below: The Walthers Warren-type through truss bridge kit is very close to the bridge the NKP used to span the Wabash River east of Cayuga, Ind., but is one panel shorter. This allowed me to model all four spans, whereas using bridges with five panels would have forced me to use only three spans in the available space, a much more noticeable deviation.

5

I kitbashed the towering Swift (now ADM) soybean-processing plant at Frankfort, Ind., using Walthers cement plant kit parts. The silos are about half as tall as the prototype's; modeling them to scale would have overpowered the scene and extended them up behind the fascia/valance of the upper deck and well into the curve forced by the end of the railroad room.

Nickel Plate's crossing of the Wabash River a few miles east of my former hometown, Cayuga, Ind. By using the Walthers single-track through-truss bridge kit, a Warren truss design with four panels instead of the prototype's five, I was able to include all four spans, **4**. Kitbashing or scratchbuilding five-panel bridges would have resulted in a three-span bridge, which in my opinion would have been a much more noticeable deviation from the prototype.

Structure height

The single large industry on my railroad is the Swift (now ADM) soybean-processing plant at the west end of the yard in Frankfort, Ind. Modeling it accurately was important

for both visual and operational standpoints.

The plant's numerous silos sent me scurrying for one of Walthers' many kits that include silos to store cement, sand, gravel, or grain. I had a cement plant kit on hand, and that quickly became the basis for the soybean plant. But when I did some digging and discovered the actual height of the prototype silos, it was clear that the kit parts were woefully short of that mark.

The good news was when I placed the kit silo moldings against the backdrop, they stood tall and appeared to have enough visual presence to suggest their much-more-massive prototypes. Better yet, they fit into the space I had reserved for the bean plant.

Now that the plant is in full

operation and most of the basic scenery around the plant is in place, **5**, I'm comfortable that I made the right judgment call. The plant does indeed look like a suitable destination for the cuts of 40-foot bean-laden boxcars that stream in daily from almost every town on the modeled Third Subdivision of the St. Louis Division.

Coping with roundhouses

After building two roundhouses from well-engineered plastic kits, I take my hat off to those of you who have scratchbuilt roundhouses. Getting all of those beams and posts and rafters and windows and doors and roof sections aligned is a pain, no two ways about it! But the end justifies the means.

6

The NKP's roundhouse at Frankfort, Ind., had 27 stalls set 7.5 degrees apart. I used a Walthers brick roundhouse kit to build my model, which has stalls spaced at 10 degrees. I was therefore able to model only 22 stalls, still more than enough to convey the appearance and to support the operational needs of the prototype. Some stalls were truncated at the aisle to ensure easy access to the turntable and radial tracks; it also provides nice views of the interior. The open end is protected by a Lexan panel. To the left (west) of the roundhouse are the truncated back shop, modeled as a shell that surrounds the engine facility control panel, and former narrow gauge car shops.

The Chesapeake & Ohio conveniently located the roundhouse at Hinton, W.Va., on the north side of the yard, putting it out of the yardmaster's way on Ted Pamperin's HO railroad. But this made the reach-in distance prohibitive, so Ted cut an opening in the wall between the workshop (former garage) and the railroad room to provide ready access for the engine hostler. *Ted Pamperin*

The biggest task was to model the NKP's 27-stall roundhouse at Frankfort, Ind., **6**. As usual, my first stop was to thumb through the Walthers catalog, and I quickly found kit 933-2900 for a brick roundhouse. Close enough, I decided.

The kit comprises three stalls, so I'd apparently need nine kits. Urp. But Walthers offers a less-expensive three-stall extension kit, which would ease the pain a bit. And a little math eased the pain a bit more: The kit stalls are set 10 degrees apart, whereas the NKP stalls were spaced at 7.5 degrees. I could fit only 22 stalls, or 7-1/3 kits, into the allocated area.

(Why not go for only 21 stalls and save the cost of an eighth extension? Where were you with these questions before I placed my order?)

As it turned out, the 22-stall roundhouse looks the part and is more than adequate for our operational needs, even though several tracks are too short to use because the stalls are truncated by the main aisle. We don't have locomotives occupying tracks as they undergo major repair work, for example.

A roundhouse is a feature attraction of any model railroad. But its large footprint and the intricacies of the associated turntable demand extremely careful planning in terms of reach-in distances for construction, maintenance, and locomotive re-railing. Some creativity may be required to simultaneously maintain prototypical accuracy and modeling practicality, **7**.

CHAPTER FOUR

Modeling detour moves

Choosing a single prototype to model among so many appealing candidates is one of the hardest choices many of us confront. I used trackage rights over the Western Maryland on my Allegheny Midland to allow some WM power to add variety, and the AM interchanged with the Virginian & Ohio and shortline Ridgeley & Midland County. My current railroad, the Nickel Plate Road, has "live" interchanges with the Chicago & Eastern Illinois, Baltimore & Ohio, Monon, and Milwaukee Road, again adding both action and variety.

Union Pacific 5903 and ex-Southern Pacific 125 head a detour move on Joe Atkinson's HO scale tribute to the Iowa Interstate, here on a former Chicago Great Western line later shared with the Rock Island through trackage rights. This scene mimics action on the full-size IAIS as UP 6672 and ex-SP 187 head west across the steel viaduct near Council Bluffs, Iowa. Such detour moves provide an opportunity to model foreign-road motive power.
Two photos: Joe Atkinson

Detour moves

Modeling detour moves is yet another way to liven things up by modeling power and even trains from another railroad. Commenting on my article, "10 tips to improve your railroad" in *Model Railroad Planning* 2015, Iowa Interstate modeler Joe Atkinson brought up the subject of detour moves:

"Detours have been such a fact of life on the Iowa Interstate over the years that I guess I've taken them for granted," Joe told me, "but they're a great way to prototypically expand the boundaries of what we can model. They often juxtaposed Union Pacific's newest locomotives against IAIS's roster, **1**, which dated to the 1950s, '60s, and '70s. Even when the detouring and host railroads are equals, detours are bound to bring an assortment of traffic and motive power types and paint schemes not normally seen on the host line.

"I've kept a list of all IAIS detours I've been aware of since the 1993 floods," Joe continued, "and while I didn't count line-by-line, it appears to be somewhere between 600 and 700

A normal day on Joe's Iowa Interstate sees a freight powered by IAIS GP38-2s (née Penn Central) in their handsome black-and-red scheme plus LLPX 2805, an ex-Reserve Mining SD38-2 leased from Locomotive Leasing Partners before being purchased by IAIS. *Joe Atkinson*

trains. Most were Union Pacific, but over the years IAIS has also hosted detours from Amtrak, Burlington Northern (or BNSF Railway), Chicago & North Western, Canadian Pacific/Soo, Southern Pacific, and I'm sure a number of others I've forgotten. My personal favorite was the June 20, 1998, Council Bluffs–Des Moines, Ia., detour of a 15-car UP office train led by their three E units."

When the detour move goes past a familiar landmark such as a bridge or depot, **2**, that makes it easier for viewers of a modeled scene to realize what's being simulated. Joe has taken advantage of the prototype's example in his modeling, and his comments got me thinking about detour moves in general. Suddenly, the light went on.

A fondness for Fs

Let's back up a step. I model the Nickel Plate Road toward the end of the steam era. Although the NKP tested a pair of EMD F7A units, they didn't make the cut. Their limited visibility to the rear during switching moves was rumored to be a factor.

Instead, the NKP ordered 10 more Berkshire (2-8-4) steam locomotives, including the celebrated 779, Lima's last domestic steam locomotive, which is now on display near its birthplace in a park in Lima, Ohio.

The NKP did purchase 11 Alco PA-1 cab units, but the remainder of the diesel road power comprised hood units from Alco, Baldwin, and EMD. The rest of the railroad industry eventually followed suit.

But from this modeler's viewpoint, the Nickel Plate's forward thinking left things a bit lacking. Ever since I got my hands on unpowered Globe (later Athearn) plastic F7 A- and B-unit kits, gleaming in their gold paint, I've been a big fan of F units. My first ride in a locomotive was in an F7, a short jaunt south on the passing track to the Rock Island depot in Sheffield, Iowa. It made a huge impression on a pre-teen's mind.

The other railroad in Sheffield was the Minneapolis & St. Louis. They, too, boasted a fleet of F units (as well as Geeps and some curious-looking and -sounding gas-electrics). Countless hours spent down by the railroad tracks built a bond between a boy and "covered wagons," as they are known.

When we moved from north-central Iowa to west-central Indiana in 1951, I beat feet down to the railroad tracks. Again, there were two railroads in town, but they crossed on diamonds rather than being parallel, as had been the case in Iowa. The Chicago & Eastern Illinois's double-track, north-south main between Chicago and Danville, Ill., and Evansville, Ind., went through my new hometown of Cayuga, Ind. The Nickel Plate Road's east-west St. Louis Division crossed the C&EI in the middle of town, **3**.

The C&EI, which also had a second main that branched off to St. Louis, thus forming an upside-down Y with Chicago at the top, offered familiar company: endless streams of Es, Fs, and Geeps, plus an occasional oddball:

one of their three EMD BL2s. It wasn't long before I got a ride in a BL2 (**3-10**) and made a new friend.

The NKP, by contrast, was all steam until the summer of 1955, save for a single rough-sounding, smoke-belching diesel that graced each of their two late-night passenger trains that made the trek between Cleveland and St. Louis. It would take a while reading *Model Railroader* and *Railroad Model Craftsman* before I realized those oddball units were Alco PA-1s, **4**, what George Hilton later dubbed "honorary steam locomotives," and he intended that comment favorably.

But nary an F graced NKP rails, save for some testing Burlington F3s

and those demonstrator F7s in the late 1940s. Thanks to Joe's offhand comment, however, that could change. On occasion, I could run a detouring C&EI Chicago-St. Louis freight behind an A-B-B-A set of Fs out of C&EI staging, around the wye at Cayuga, **5**, over the NKP's Third Subdivision, **6**, and into NKP staging at the west end of the railroad.

I was recently chatting with my good friend Ron Marquardt, a retired Monon engineer and later a Louisville & Nashville and CSX official. He recalled a Monon detour occasioned by a wreck just south of Lafayette, Ind. It took the NKP's Peoria Division southeast to Frankfort, then the NKP's

The Chicago & Eastern Illinois' Chicago-Evansville, Ind., main line crossed the NKP's St. Louis Division in Cayuga, Ind. Here a northbound freight headed by two EMD Geeps and a BL2 hammers over the NKP main between the C&EI tower and joint depot and Fable House Hotel.

4

St. Louis Division west to Linden, and backed through the NKP-Monon interchange track at Linden, Ind., thus regaining the Monon's southbound main line to Louisville, Ky. (Ron also noted that it was common to detour a wrecker over another railroad to bring it around a derailment so both ends

of the wreck could be worked by the home carrier.)

I could do the same thing with Monon F3s and/or maybe a BL2, Alco RS-2, or F-M H15-44—all available factory-painted for the Monon—using my Peoria Division and Linden staging tracks, **7**.

Any detour move would add some interesting operational challenges. I shouldn't, and couldn't, just surprise my dispatcher and crews with such detour moves, as—for example—the C&EI staging track leading to the C&EI-NKP interchange track at Cayuga isn't long enough to "hide" an entire train.

"Extra C&EI NNN West." Lacking orders giving it special rights, finding a time slot for it to move would be up to the crew and akin to moving any extra over the subdivision: It's inferior to all eastbound trains, and it has to clear westbound first-class train No. 9 five minutes ahead of the departure time at the closest station to its rear where time is shown in the employee timetable.

Once it works its way over the railroad to the division point yard at Charleston, Ill., the pilot/road crew would get off, and a new crew would take over for the remainder of the run to home rails—that is, into one of my west-end staging tracks. My road crews never deal with moves in or out of hidden staging; those moves are handled by a designated operator. In my experience, dealing with staging can quickly diminish the realism of an otherwise prototypical run over the main line.

Home-road lead units

I was discussing detour moves with Chuck Conway, one of my primary resources for Colorado-area photography. He sent several photos showing Denver & Rio Grande Western detours over the Union Pacific, all with a UP unit leading, 8. "UP units had cab signals whose indications followed the lineside signals," Chuck told me, "a handy thing when fog, blizzards, or a burned-out signal light made lineside signals hard or impossible to see.

"Rio Grande had eight SD45s so equipped," he added, "and they could lead the Kaiser Steel coal trains while on the UP between Provo, Utah, and

Rather, the C&EI detour move would, as 5 shows, be partially out onto NKP tracks as the session began.

And it would be facing east, whereas to regain C&EI tracks leading to St. Louis, it would have to run west. So a runaround move at Cayuga would be the first order of business. In the real world, the C&EI crew would be accompanied by an NKP pilot, but that's not needed, although I'm sure Chief Dispatcher Jim Schweitzer would be hovering around this train for its run over the western half of the Third Subdivision.

The detour move would become

An A-B-A set of Chicago & Eastern Illinois F units eases around the interchange wye at Cayuga, Ind., as this southbound freight detours over the Nickel Plate owing to a derailment on the C&EI's St. Louis line. The units will have to run around their train, then head southwest to regain C&EI rails at Mode, Ill. In reality, they are coming off the interchange staging track at Cayuga and will end their run on an NKP Fourth Sub staging track.

A later detour move saw a C&EI EMD FP7-F3 consist on the head end of another westbound freight as it climbed the 1.29 percent grade of Cayuga Hill on the deck girder bridge over the Little Vermilion River near the Indiana-Illinois state line. It will run over the Illinois half of the modeled NKP Third Subdivision.

7 I can simulate a Monon detour move between Lafayette and Louisville by staging a Monon freight on an NKP Peoria Division staging track and have the staging crew run it into Frankfort. A Third Sub "pilot crew" can then take it west over the St. Louis Division to Linden, Ind., and back it into the Monon delivery track, a 30-car-long hidden staging track.

8 On June 24, 1983, a derailment on the Rio Grande resulted in Union Pacific SD40-2 3676 leading D&RGW GP30 3007 and a tunnel motor on train No. 100 (Chicago-Oakland trailers) on a detour over the Union Pacific through Peckham, Colo. A UP lead unit was required because of onboard cab-signaling equipment. *Chuck Conway*

9

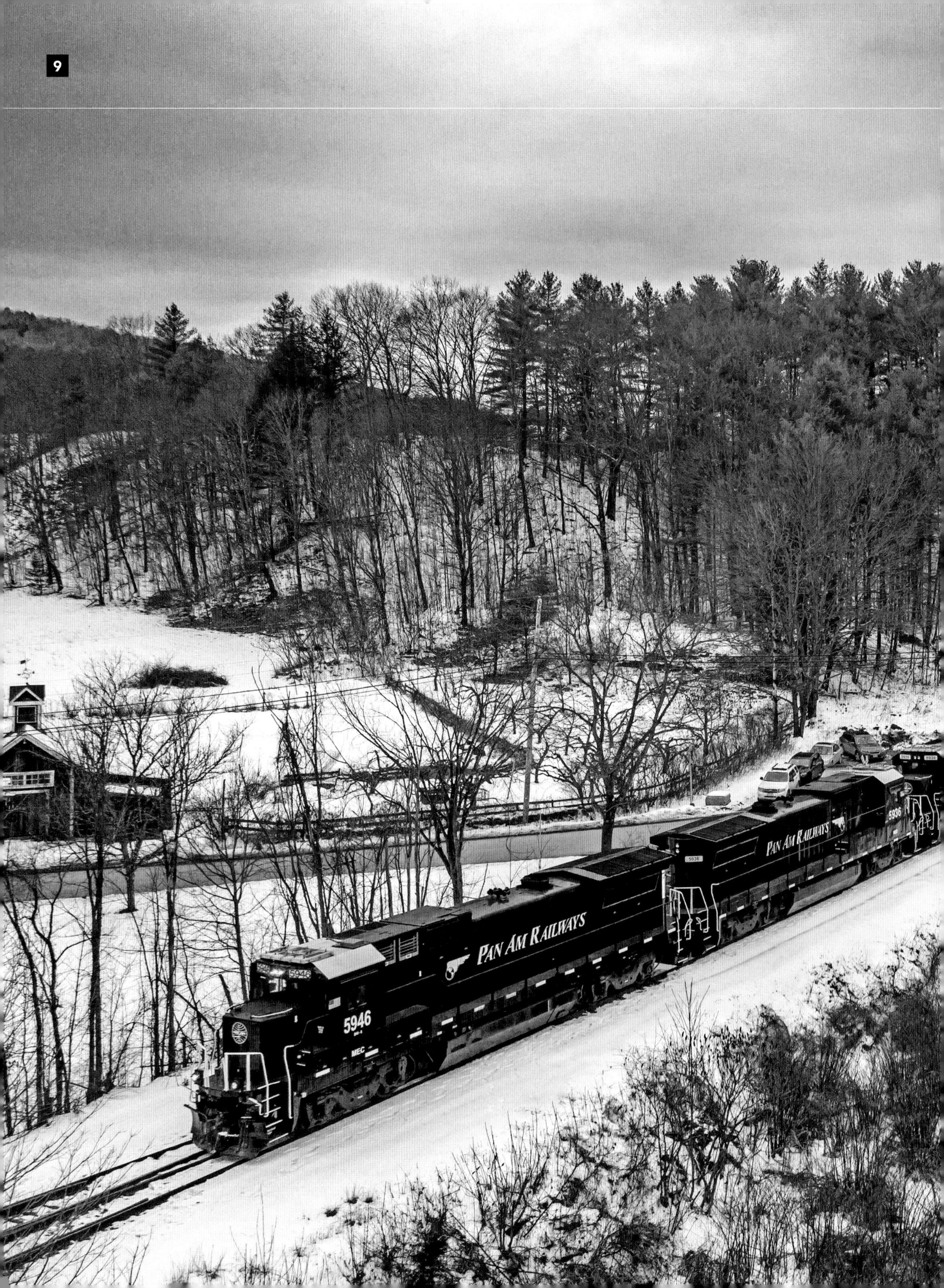

Following the partial collapse of a portion of Pan Am Railway's famous 4.75-mile-long Hoosac Tunnel, arrangements were made to keep the Binghamton, N.Y.-East Deerfield, Mass., trains fluid by detouring over neighboring Vermont Rail System. On February 16, 2020, train 16R is eastbound passing the 2012-rebuilt Bartonsville, Vt., covered bridge on VRS's Green Mountain Railroad's Bellows Falls Subdivision with a quartet of Pan Am GE B40-8s plus VTR EMD GP40-2 303 and GP40-2L 310. *Kevin Burkholder*

10

Fontana, Calif. Chicago & North Western had a lot of their newer units so equipped, and they also regularly led while on the UP."

A modern example of motive power variety was provided when Pan Am Railways ran detour moves over the Vermont Railway System, **9**, following a partial tunnel collapse.

Using a prototype photo as the basis for modeling a scene is an excellent way to apply lessons from the prototype, including detour moves, as Phil Keppers has done on his HO Northern Pacific layout, **10**. Phil spotted the photo of a scene at Stampede Pass, Wash., in a book by the late Jim Frederickson.

"During an operating session," Phil reports, "if I have enough crew members, in the morning I dispatch a light four-unit FT from Auburn (the west staging yard) up across Stampede Pass to Easton. There the Milwaukee's *Olympian Hiawatha* is pulled onto the NP and run as the second section of the *North Coast Limited* (or, if it's too late for that, it is run as an extra) and pulled across Stampede Pass down to Auburn. In the afternoon, the sequence is reversed. It's an interesting operation that allows for some flexibility depending on how many people I have available to operate, and it allows me an excuse to run an electric locomotive on my otherwise strictly NP layout."

Modeling a scene from a prototype photo is an excellent way to apply lessons from the prototype, as it provides a benchmark for comparison. Phil Keppers is still building his HO scale Northern Pacific but is already able to judge his efforts by depicting a 1949 detour of a Milwaukee Road *Hiawatha* over the Northern Pacific based on a photo in Jim Frederickson's book, *Steam to Diesel*. **Jim took the photo at Stampede, Wash., between Tunnels 3 and 4.** *Model photo: Jim Ramnes; prototype photo: Jim Fredrickson, JMF20-06300.0, NPRHA Collection at Burien, Wash.*

CHAPTER FIVE

Variety through used and foreign-road equipment

The variety evident in July 1963 at Louisville & Nashville's South Louisville (Ky.) Shops was enhanced when the railroad dabbled in the used-locomotive market by acquiring Alco cab and hood units from the recently abandoned Lehigh & New England (the FA, middle) and Rutland (RS-3, right).
Charles B. Castner

As builders of railroad empires, be they large, medium or small in stature, we need to take advantage of every time, labor, and money-saving device they and we can lay our hands on. Even the full-size railroads aren't above grabbing a bargain when they see one—no sense spending money on something new when something used will do the job. We can also benefit from some visual variety in our equipment rosters without stretching plausibility if we play our cards right.

2

Randy Laframboise and Mike Sparks are building a superb multi-deck HO scale tribute to the Rutland (see *Model Railroad Planning 2016*). Randy recently painted and lettered this New England Rail Service brass model of the Rutland's 600-hp GE 70-tonner. The prototype was purchased in 1951 for use as a yard and industry switcher for Rutland, Vt. It was sold to the Clarendon & Pittsford RR in 1963 and the Kelley's Creek & Northwestern in 1972. *Randy Laframboise*

Second-hand equipment

The Louisville & Nashville apparently needed some motive power about the time the Lehigh & New England and the Rutland ceased operations in the early 1960s. They picked up several L&NE Alco FAs and RS-2s and Rutland RS-3s at bargain prices, as the mid-1963 photo attests, **1**. Here's a chance to model the power of two very popular Northeastern railroads in an equally popular Appalachian setting.

West Virginia short line Kelley's Creek & Northwestern also did that by acquiring a former Rutland GE 70-tonner, **2**. And the Tennessee Railroad acquired six second-hand Alco RS-1s, including former Rutland 400, and adopted its handsome yellow-striped green paint scheme. I followed their example when I relettered some Atlas RS-1s that had been factory-painted for the Rutland for my Ridgeley & Midland County short line, **3**, which connected to the Allegheny Midland at Midland, W.Va.

To maintain plausibility, if that's a concern, keep timing in mind. The scenario illustrated here works only

3

Like the prototype Tennessee Railroad, my freelanced Ridgeley & Midland County acquired former Rutland Alco RS-1s (mine came from Atlas). I simply painted over the old lettering before adding new reporting marks, road number, and diamond-shaped R&MC herald.

The South Shore, the Milwaukee Road, and a Brazilian railroad benefited when the delivery of an order for 2-D+D-2 electrics built for Russia was canceled by the U.S. government. Three of them joined rebuilt ex-New York Central boxcabs and powered South Shore freights until electric freight service was terminated.

for the early 1960s. Before 1960, these locomotives weren't available; not long after that, they were either retired or repainted into L&N's livery.

The Chicago South Shore & South Bend ran its freight operations for decades with second-hand power, first with rebuilt ex-New York Central R-2 boxcabs, **4**. They complemented those

with a trio of 2-D+D-2 streamlined electrics originally built in 1949 by General Electric to 5-foot gauge for Stalinist Russia, **5**. Five more went to Brazil, and the Milwaukee Road got the remaining dozen. Powering a freelanced electric road with the five that went to South America wouldn't be a huge stretch. Add to those some

5

4 The Chicago South Shore & South Bend's shop forces were fully capable of turning worn-out New York Central R-2 boxcabs into the 700-series motors they needed to supplement some light steeple-cab locomotives that dated to the 1920s. Some of these were in turn rebuilt into even more modern boxcabs in the 1960s.

cast-off Pennsylvania, Boston & Maine, Great Northern, or Virginian electrics, and you're in the circa-1950s or '60s freight-hauling business under the overhead.

Mergers present a similar opportunity to add visual variety. I have been considering an era shift to model the Nickel Plate as it existed in the early 1960s prior to its October 1964 merger into the Norfolk & Western. Then it dawned on me that if I modeled the months up to perhaps a year shortly after the merger, I could add a Wabash F7 or General Electric U25B to a consist, **6**, or maybe even an N&W high-hood Alco Century 420 or one of those odd-looking high-hood GP30s. Pure NKP consists would still be the norm, but the opportunity to do some interesting foreign-road models would be at hand.

By modeling an immediate post-merger era, consist variety is easily achieved. Above, a timetable-eastward freight heads north through Springfield, Ill., on May 19, 1965, seven months after the Wabash and NKP merged into the Norfolk & Western. Leading is Wabash U25B 511 and F7 648, both in their original paint schemes, plus repainted N&W F7 3717 (former WAB 717). The merger also found power from the three railroads consisted (inset).
Springfield photo: J. David Ingles

Mainline power is relegated to branch or short lines as more modern locomotives join the roster. Norfolk & Western's once-mighty Mastodon 4-8-0s saw service on several Virginia short lines; 375 is on Train 111 on the Blacksburg Branch (above). Number 475 was restored to service at Strasburg, Pa. (left), another example of how modelers can use former Class 1 power in more modest settings.
Above: Parker Hayden;
Left: Larry DeYoung

7

Steam power

Steam locomotives were hard to kill. Like George Washington's hatchet, almost anything that wore out could be and was replaced, allowing locomotives built at the turn of the century to see service until the end of steam. Some of them are going strong today.

As steel underframes replaced truss rods and then steel cars debuted, trains grew heavier and longer. Locomotives grew as well; engines that were once the pride of the fleet became local power and then were to relegated to branch lines or sold to short lines.

An interesting example: Norfolk & Western's once mighty 4-8-0s became famous working branch lines after they caught the eye of gifted photographer O. Winston Link. Remarkably, one of them, No. 475, **7**, steams today at Strasburg, Pa., thanks to a remarkable resurrection by the highly skilled steam shop team led by Linn Moedinger at the Strasburg Rail Road.

Examples of steam power moving around like hobos abound. With a bit of discretion, ample opportunities exist for employing previously owned steam on your railroad. The smaller the scope

of your railroad, the more likely it would be to tap into the used market.

And you can't go wrong by adopting a fleet of new or second-hand United States Railroad Administration (USRA) steam power, as I discussed in *Time-saving Techniques for Building Model Railroads* (Kalmbach, 2019). A good example is the Akron, Canton & Youngstown. The AC&Y acquired four USRA light Mikados (2-8-2s) from the NKP, numbering them 407-410. Chris Lantz models the AC&Y in HO and acquired several of the Key imports based on the 400s, **8**.

Chris Lantz reports that Akron, Canton & Youngstown's four ex-NKP USRA 2-8-2s were used to support the Mikes they already owned and often double-headed on heavy trains. The AC&Y had doghouses for the head brakeman on the tenders of all of their Mikados. Number 408 is ex-Nickel Plate 616 (above). Chris used a Key brass import of a USRA light Mikado to model AC&Y 407 (below). *Prototype photo: Chris Lantz collection; model photo: Chris Lantz*

8

Following the abandonment of the Rock Island in 1980, the Allegheny Midland acquired some boxcars in the ROCK paint scheme, applied AM reporting marks, and put them to work. They added visual variety and interest with very little extra effort, although I did update them by removing the running boards and adding roller-bearing trucks, consolidated and U-1 wheel stencils, and Automatic Car Identification tags.

A number of other NKP light Mikes headed southwest to Mexico (one could assume they headed to your railroad instead), so geographic restraints are not a major concern when it comes to finding new homes for used USRA power.

Repurposing also applies to rolling stock. Following the failure of the Rock Island in 1980, I assumed the Allegheny Midland acquired some Rock Island boxcars and changed the reporting marks, **9**.

Such "patch" jobs are offered commercially by various model manufacturers from time to time.

Variety, the spice of life

It's difficult to whittle our interests down to a single railroad. A lot of freelancing is really nothing more than

The truncated Chicago & Eastern Illinois double-track main line at Cayuga, Ind., is long enough for a northbound local crew to work Thompson's elevator and the NKP interchange as well as for a southbound passenger train to move from hidden staging up to the depot, make a station stop, and—when no one is looking—be moved back into staging.

11

The Monon interchanges with the Nickel Plate at Frankfort (above) and Linden, Ind., on my railroad. Frankfort's interchange is merely a stubbed-off wye located out of view to the left of this photo; the truncated Monon-Indianapolis main line is visible at right and the freight house, with a boxcar on its isolated track, is at right. The parked RS-2 on the Monon main helps illustrate what's going on.

12

The NKP-Monon interchange at Linden, like the MILW interchange at Humrick (next page), is automated using Iowa Scale Engineering's Automated Interchange circuitry. The interchange track is more than 30 cars long, and a pair of Monon units shoves new cuts of about 8 cars into view as each cut is picked up by a passing NKP through freight. The infrared sensor that will shut off power to the Monon units is just to the left of the Pennsylvania boxcar.

Adding visual variety to the otherwise all-NKP roster on my railroad is accomplished in part by posing a Milwaukee Road caboose on the stub-ended track that crosses the NKP's St. Louis Division at the Milwaukee's interlocking tower at Humrick, Ill. (above). Behind the low backdrop the caboose is butted up against is a 30-car stub-ended staging track that allows a pair of MILW Fairbanks-Morse C-Liners to deliver a series of cuts of cars to the NKP using Iowa Scaled Engineering's Automated Interlocking circuitry (below). When the last cut of about 8 cars is delivered and picked up, the FMs ease into view, cover an infrared sensor, and shut themselves off.

13

an admission that we want to choose something from column A ... and perhaps column B, and maybe columns C and D.

Even those of us who profess to limit our modeling interests to a single railroad—the Nickel Plate Road in my case—usually build in some form of a Plan B, and maybe C and D too. The subdivision I chose to model interchanges with quite a few "foreign roads," including two personal favorites: the Monon and the Chicago & Eastern Illinois. This allows me to have fleets of cars from both railroads that are interchanged with the NKP.

Enough of the C&EI has been modeled at Cayuga, Ind., for me to employ a C&EI local crew to work a grain elevator and the NKP interchange, plus move a passenger train in and out of staging, **10**. As I describe in Chapter 4, I can even orchestrate a C&EI detour move over the NKP now and then (**4-5**).

At Frankfort, Ind., Monon power is limited to what I can pose on the stubbed-off main line segment by the NKP roundhouse, **11**. But at Linden, Ind., a pair of Monon units, **12**, shows up now and then after they have delivered the last cut of interchange cars to the NKP from a hidden 30-car "live" interchange track that employs

Iowa Scaled Engineering's Automated Interchange circuitry.

The same thing happens at Humrick, Ill. I spotted a Milwaukee Road caboose on the 16" length of Milwaukee main line to remind NKP crews with whom they're interchanging there, **13**. A pair of Fairbanks-Morse C-Liners pop out from behind a view block after they deliver the final cut of NKP interchange cars.

I could also pose a New York Central locomotive and a car or two on the former Big Four double-track main that crosses the NKP at Charleston, Ill. And a Baltimore & Ohio local behind one or two EMD GP7s, **14**, comes out of staging to do some interchange work at Metcalf, Ill., a live interchange that—like the C&EI at Cayuga— requires a live crew member to operate.

Visual variety achieved

I'm sure you can think of other ways to achieve some visual variety that isn't as simplistic as buying one of these and one of those simply because the model appeals to you—although I do admit doing just that on occasion. There are prototypically plausible reasons to model more than one railroad's equipment on even a very small railroad. Perhaps an example I have shared here helps you to do that.

14

Unlike the automated interchanges at Linden and Humrick, the Baltimore & Ohio interchange at Metcalf, Ill., requires a live operator to deliver and pick up cars from and to the NKP using a pair of 700-series EMD GP7s. The local, which initially fouls the NKP main line as the day begins, switches the interchange, then continues into hidden staging.

CHAPTER SIX

Choosing a prototype— or base prototype

The most basic concern facing anyone trying to apply the principles of prototype railroading to scale modeling is choosing a railroad to model. Today's plethora of accurately detailed, great-running models gives us more choices while making it even harder to choose just one from Column A or Column B. Perhaps looking beyond the mainstream solutions and applying a little creativity—doing some carefully considered freelancing, modeling an obscure short or branch line, simplifying complex tasks, doing more with less—will help.

Left: Train No. 11, the *Laker*, arrives at the Atlantic Great Eastern's depot in South Dover, Maine. AGE steam locomotives follow practices of parent Canadian National; Mikado 3761 has the V-shaped number boards and tilted wafer herald on the tender. The standard paint scheme gives the depot (built by Jack Tyson following plans of the Ann Arbor depot at Owosso, Mich.) and adjacent freight house (built by Craig Wilson) a family resemblance. Jack Ozanich's AGE is a superb example of the potential of prototype-based freelancing. *Craig Wilson*

Allagash Railway's Madrid Engine Terminal is jammed with power on a gray day in April 1985. If you look closely, you will also note power from Guilford-family roads Maine Central and Delaware & Hudson. *Mike Confalone*

I'll go on record as saying that I consider the better examples of prototype-based freelancing—some examples being Jack Ozanich's Atlantic Great Eastern, **1**; Mike Confalone's Allagash, **2**; Bill Darnaby's Maumee Route, **3**; Eric Brooman's Utah Belt, **4**; Allen McClelland's Virginian & Ohio, **1-3**; and anything Paul Dolkos chooses to do, **5**—as forms of prototype modeling. The knowledge of full-size railroad practices and skill that went into these railroads exceeds that of most prototype-based model railroads.

So, no, freelancing has not and will not go out of style. It's a matter of degree and always has been.

Good prototype modeling, like

3

Bill Darnaby took prototype-based freelancing to another level by applying the Maumee Route as an overlay to Ohio's railroad network. Here the Maumee was superimposed on an actual New York Central (Big Four and Toledo & Ohio Central) crossing at Edison, Ohio. This allowed Bill do some actual prototype modeling, here of a New York Central tower instead of a Maumee-style tower, thus helping to anchor the roots of his freelanced railroad. *Bill Darnaby*

good prototype-based freelancing, requires a lot of due diligence. So it's not so much a matter of choosing a specific prototype that you like as much as it is one that you enjoy researching, one that is well supported by a railroad-specific historical society, and one that has a solid base of manufacturing support (unless you really enjoy taking the road less traveled).

So one's first task isn't so much to choose a railroad to model but to come to grips with one's level of investment in the project. I recently read an interesting column in *Road & Track* magazine by a hot-shoe editor who was a little tired of hearing from strangers that they, too, always wanted to become race-car drivers. "No they didn't," he thought to himself, "or they would have become one. They lacked the drive and motivation and sacrifice required to become racecar drivers."

So it is with railroad empire builders. Better we find out in advance that we lack one or more of the key elements required to emulate one of our heroes who has erected a basement-size railroad or two. Once we have settled on something reasonable, then and only then can we choose a prototype to model.

Thinking medium or small rather than large doesn't mean abandoning a Class 1 railroad. Many Class 1s had very appealing branch lines. Jared Harper models an obscure branch line of the mighty, far-flung Santa Fe, **6**, one that suits his building and operating pace and tastes. He wisely determined that this branch was within his grasp before he started on a more ambitious project that would have resulted in failure. He described it in *Model Railroad Planning* 2009.

"I model Santa Fe's 33-mile-long Alma branch in eastern Kansas in a

Eric Brooman's Utah Belt is unique in that he has always worked hard to keep the railroad up to date. I clearly recall UB freights powered by F units when the railroad occupied a bi-level house's basement. The new UB features the latest motive power and rolling stock in the Broomans' more spacious new home. The skillfully rendered paint scheme and scenery make it easy to expect one would encounter a full-size Utah Belt while driving through the Beehive State.

Eric Brooman

4

Paul Dolkos once modeled a slightly freelanced Boston & Maine layout set in New Hampshire (above), but now models the Baltimore, Md., harbor area (right). Everything looks the part, but Paul doesn't allow Reality to get in the way of Practicality, yet he never compromises on Plausibility. *Paul Dolkos*

22'-6" by 30'-0" area," Jared reports. "I have about 150 feet of mainline track with 22 turnouts. During my operating sessions, which last about three hours, we run mixed trains 95/96 from Burlingame to Alma and back. We use prototype paperwork, and the operation is based on interviews with the members of the train crews from the 1940s and '50s. We switch cars going westbound and pick up cars coming back eastbound. Train crews comprise an engineer, conductor, and brakeman." Rounding up even two or three crewmembers is enough of a challenge, he reports.

"People who come to operate on my railroad enjoy the slow pace of operations; many are regulars. Most of the operation is in the towns, but there is a fair amount of main [branch] line running."

Jared's railroad is relatively large but certainly not what I'd call complex. So

large doesn't have to mean complex. My railroad is roughly 30 x 60 feet in size, comprises two division-point yards with staging beyond them, and is multi-deck, which makes it complex by any measure. But in that same footprint, one could have modeled a single-track out-and-back branch line, perhaps in S or O or even large scale, on a single deck, and have had a very basic, simple-yet-rewarding railroad.

I'm picturing one of the Milwaukee's or Burlington's granger branches in Iowa or Minnesota—think amber waves of grain, of towering sentinels of the prairies in the form of grain elevators and lonely depots, of 2-8-0s or 4-6-0s, or Geeps or those unique Milwaukee SDL39s.

Wow!

Experience counts

We all have stories to tell about great plans that came up short. This seems

to be a special peril for prototype modelers as we seriously contemplate gymnasium-size layouts, modeling entire divisions of a major railroad, even winning the lottery to make such dreams affordable. Perhaps the most surprising thing is that some of us actually manage to pull off such grandiose plans.

But for every success story, there are scores of tales of half-completed benchwork with nary a length of powered track on which to run still-boxed trains. Successful prototype modeling isn't about size but about setting goals that are attainable before the fires that begat them die out.

When I first contemplated modeling the Third Subdivision of the former Nickel Plate Road's St. Louis Division, that set in motion a plethora of plans that, in hindsight, were a bit over the top. For example, once I had defined not only the subdivision but

Jared Harper models the Santa Fe, but not Cajon Pass or Raton Pass or any of the railroad's other famous scenes. Instead, to keep his quest manageable, he models a Kansas branch line. But even this relatively simple branch took three skilled operators "a record time" of 2:15 to work from Burlingame to Alma and back. Consider: In Eskridge was Clinton L. Scott Lumber with coal bins, warehouse, granary, unloading platform, sand bin, stockyard, Phillips 66, Standard Oil, and Sinclair. No. 95, the westbound daily-except-Sunday mixed with 2-6-0 No. 9441, is setting out a tank car of gasoline at the Standard Oil penstock (above). From there they went westbound with an LCL car and two stock cars of cattle to be unloaded at Hessdale (top right). The long stock train is Extra 9441 West passing through Harveyville on the way to Hessdale (bottom right). *Three photos: Jared Harper*

6

also specific towns to model, how hard could it be to drive along that 110 miles of railroad and shoot digital photos to use on the backdrop?

It was practical to do this in select locations such as sites where major streets or highways crossed the NKP. Removing modern signage and vehicles wasn't that hard using photo-editing software—Photoshop Elements in my case—and some building fronts and sides could be backdated, **7**.

To do this for every foot of backdrop, however, was a very bad idea. For starters, a lot has changed since 1954—new structures have been built or old ones torn down, modernized, or abandoned; forests now appear where fields once reigned supreme; and the Third Sub itself was abandoned in 1989 save for a section near Charleston, Ill., now operated by shortline Eastern Illinois Railroad.

I settled for shooting only key areas and using commercial backdrops, most from SceniKing, to fill in the long runs between towns, **8**.

Whoa, Nellie!

When it comes to choosing a prototype to model, sticking to his objectives, and producing an excellent model railroad, my good friend and neighbor, Perry Squier, is one of the best examples I can think of. His dad was a model railroader, and he had some experience as a club member. But decades passed before he built his lifetime home and had a basement for his dream railroad.

In search of that dream railroad, he stumbled across an article by Bob Schleicher in *Model Railroading* magazine about a down-on-its-heels short line in northwestern Pennsylvania and southwestern New York called the Pittsburg, Shawmut & Northern that looked appealing. He started to build Bob's track plan, called in some veteran modelers, including me, for advice, was told he was wasn't using his available space as fully as he could, and started over.

His second effort was surprisingly sophisticated for a relative newcomer to track planning and prototype

modeling, and the resulting railroad has proven to be a remarkable tribute to the Shawmut as it appeared in 1923, **9**, and a lot of fun to operate.

But midway toward his goal, he almost made two major mistakes. Both involved assuming he needed a bigger railroad. When he built his home, only half of the area under it was excavated for a basement, so he pondered whether it would be practical to have the other half dug out. Radiant heating in the floor suggested that any sagging and cracking there would incur a very high penalty, so that was aborted.

Plan B was to build a 40 x 70-foot barn on his ample property. It was sized to accommodate a track plan meeting his every desire, especially a couple of key Shawmut scenes he had to omit, and to substantially lengthen the runs between towns on this timetable and train-order railroad. Downstairs would be several horse stalls, as wife Kathy is an international horse-show judge and at the time dealt with brokering horse sales.

The barn got built. I clearly recall

A recent photo of Veedersburg's Second Street was backdated using Photoshop Elements by "painting over" modern vehicles and signs using the clone (rubber stamp) tool. But I should have added 1940s and '50s vehicles from other digital sources before printing out the resulting image for use on my backdrop. Now I'll have to add them by the old cut-and-paste method.

7

Most of my backdrops are from SceniKing except for in-town scenes where I have spliced in actual photos that have been backdated. I usually trim off the sky from the commercial backdrops. I then alter the tree line and section out or paste over distinctive structures so I can repeatedly reuse the same scene.

When is half a basement better than a full basement? When a full basement would accommodate too much railroad to allow detailing it to the desired degree, as Perry Squier discovered as work on his 1923 Pittsburg, Shawmut & Northern has progressed. The result is a highly detailed representation of the railroad as it existed in a narrowly defined timeframe. Here handsome Mogul No. 21 heads north to Olean, N.Y., in 1923, its last year of operation.

ascending the stairs to the loft where Shawmut 2.0 was intended to reside. A single 100-watt bulb hung on a cable from the ceiling. When turned on, a few photons managed to bounce off the closest walls. Man, that was a large haymow!

It didn't take long for Perry to realize that the idea of coming home from work (he's now retired), trudging out to the barn on a cold, dark evening, and working on the new railroad when he had a perfectly good one in his basement that still needed a lot of

work was not a reasonable thing to do.

But the story ends well. Kathy acquired a horse of her own, so the barn is being put to good use. I borrowed the loft for a photo shoot when I built a large-scale project railroad for *Model Railroader*, which explains why two walls in one corner are painted sky blue. And Perry is diligently scratchbuilding or carefully kitbashing every building that was down by the railroad tracks in every town that he had room to model in his basement. So his half-basement

empire has turned out to be the most reasonable goal of all.

He chose a relatively obscure prototype to model, one that demanded a tremendous amount of due diligence. Along the way, he made many new friends, enjoyed numerous road trips to the area where the railroad once operated, and has become one of the leading experts on the Pittsburg, Shawmut & Northern.

Isn't that what a hobby is ideally all about?

1

CHAPTER SEVEN

Modeling as a time machine

One of the recurrent themes in my talks and writings is how a prototype-based scale model railroad is one of the closest approximations of a time machine, a lens that allows us to peer back into time, ever devised. Until virtual reality allows us to venture into a computer-generated past of our own choosing—and I doubt that re-creating my favorite stretch of railroad in my preferred modeling era is going to be high on any developer's list—building a 1:160 or 1:87 or whatever scale model railroad and operating it realistically remains our best bet.

Jack Burgess models the Yosemite Valley in HO scale as it appeared in August 1939. Although Jack does not shy away from scratchbuilding almost anything in any scale, he has benefited from commercial support. In the photo at left with a train passing scratchbuilt Merced station, No. 25 is a brass 2-6-0 imported by Beaver Creek; Jack supplied the drawings. The RPO is a brass import from Overland Models, one of four importers of this car. The photos above and at right show views of the park entrance at El Portal that today can be viewed only as a scene on a model railroad. *Jack Burgess*

A lifelong quest

Jack Burgess is well known for his faithful depiction of California's Yosemite Valley RR in HO scale as it appeared in August 1939, **1**. Why 1939? One of the reasons that Jack originally selected that particular year to model was the availability of a brass model of Railway Post Office car 107, which was purchased by the YV two years earlier. That model, imported by Ken Kidder, is crude by today's standards but was the only brass model available for modeling the YV at the time.

But Jack quickly discovered that sitting by the mailbox hoping what he needed would show up was not a successful strategy. Jack, a civil engineer, provided plans and photos to importer Beaver Creek for five YV locomotives. That may not be a practical tactic for most of us, but we can do our part by gathering information that a manufacturer or importer will need to paint and letter an existing model or even to produce a new model. Working with other like-minded modelers through railroad-specific historical societies is almost always the best approach. Compare this to sending a manufacturer or importer a "Why don't you make …?" email or letter.

In Jack's case, his decades of due diligence and museum-quality modeling have produced a means for us to travel back to the time just before World War II when the Yosemite Valley was still hauling tourists by the carload to America's natural Disneyland, incomparable Yosemite National Park.

From the Rockies to Maine

Andrew Dodge's basement has long been a portal to a previous time in the Centennial State. Until not that long ago, one could visit his authentic re-creation of the Denver, South Park & Pacific in On3.

2

It's September 27, 1897, and Colorado Midland train No. 6, the *Kansas City and Chicago Limited,* arrived late off the Second Division from Grand Junction, Colo. Engine No. 4 will take charge of the train for its trip on the First Division to Colorado Springs and connections east. *Andrew Dodge*

As we reported in *Model Railroad Planning* 2015 and before that in 2013, Andrew dismantled the South Park in favor of another bold venture back in time, on this occasion to revisit the fabled Colorado Midland. He liked the bulk of O scale (1:48, or ¼" to the foot) modeling, and the CM, being standard gauge, **2**, would have even more heft than the DSP&P equipment.

Precise historian and modeler that he is, however, O gauge's incorrect 5-foot gauge would not do. So Andrew looked to O fine-scale, what we call Proto:48, where the distance between the rails is not only the correct 4'-8½" but the wheel profile is also correctly based on prototype standards.

Never mind that zilch was available

to support his newfound quest. He'd simply scratchbuild what he needed, including a roster of steam locomotives. And so he did, rivaling the best models that have come across the Pacific.

So what did he get for his efforts? We can start by assuming he derived a vast amount of satisfaction. One neglects to give proper emphasis to the word "model" in the term "model railroading" at considerable peril. Modeling—that is, actually building models—is as enjoyable and rewarding as it ever was.

In fact, the latest reports from Andrew indicate his basement is virtually moving from Colorado to Down East Maine where abundant new modeling challenges and

Some of us have the skills and motivation to build almost anything we can't buy. One such modeler is Andrew Dodge, who built the required fleet of O fine-scale (Proto:48) locomotives to power his Colorado Midland trains and the railroad to run them on. He is now converting the locomotives for use in a Down East setting. He's staying in the same 1890s time period but will modify his current layout from the Rocky Mountains to coastal Maine between Belfast and nearby Deer Island. Side-wheeler *Mt. Desert Isle* will travel between them to serve the upper echelon of society during the summer months, and a tugboat and its car float will transport railroad traffic. *Andrew Dodge*

3

opportunities await him, **3**. He's not about to scrap that hard-won fleet of Colorado Midland steam power, of course, so you can bet that whatever he chooses to do will be another venture back in time that allows him to visit a familiar place during an unfamiliar time period when vintage steam still ruled the high iron.

Today, with such superb support from both brass importers and the makers of what we loosely term "plastic" models, it's relatively easy to do a credible job of modeling a specific prototype without doing much modeling—unless you choose to model the likes of the Colorado Midland in P:48, of course. That allows us to move from concept to realistic operation at a rapid rate. It also facilitates missing out on one of the more satisfying aspects of our broad-shouldered hobby: model building.

A good friend of mine, Jared Harper, who models a Santa Fe branch line in HO scale (**6-6** and MRP 2009), has often stated that he would be quite happy to be able to go from planning to operation in no time flat. He sees the railroad-building steps between here and there as necessary evils, this despite the fact that he is an accomplished scratchbuilder who takes time to do his homework and build highly accurate models, **4**.

I understand his viewpoint. But I also suspect that he, like Andrew, gets a lot of pleasure out of sharing his modeling prowess with the rest of us via articles and displays at prototype-modeling meets.

In any event, both gentlemen have built credible replicas in miniature of specific locales at narrowly defined times. Thanks to their considerable efforts, the rest of us are afforded the opportunity to join them on a trip back in time.

Their examples serve as a testimonial to the potential of scale model railroading. Most of us won't fully realize that potential, and I'm sure both of these modelers will admit to coming up short in some aspects of their quest for a perfect representation of a given time and place.

This suggests that the quest is perhaps equally or even more enjoyable than the realization of that effort. But as long as the result allows them, and us, to enjoy venturing back in time—decades, years, maybe only weeks—the hobby has served its purpose.

Santa Fe modeler Jared Harper said that he wouldn't mind having a railroad built to his standards and specifications and ready for operating handed to him on a silver platter, but he is also a skilled model builder and diligent researcher, as these scenes along his rural branch line attests. Every structure is a scratchbuilt homage to its prototype based on field trips, interviews, and research. *Jared Harper*

Coming home again

In a Trains of Thought commentary in the March 2019 *Model Railroader,* I discussed a project that I had been putting off because I knew it was going to be a bear: scratchbuilding a model of the L-shaped brick depot that graced the intersection of the Chicago & Eastern Illinois' Chicago-Evansville, Ind., double-track main line and the Nickel Plate Road's St. Louis Division. But there was no getting around it, as Cayuga, Ind., was my hometown for much of the 1950s and a signature location on my HO tribute to the Third Subdivision of the NKP's St. Louis line.

When we moved from Iowa to west-central Indiana in 1951, it didn't

take me long to find the crossing of the C&EI and NKP, and I spent some time with the interlocking tower operators and station agent.

The depot wasn't a bright and airy place. Rather, it had the characteristics of a medieval castle with turrets and a dark waiting room. But it was quite an edifice for a small Hoosier village that had few claims to fame other than a large grain elevator, a canning factory, a small concrete-block plant, and the brickyard my dad managed.

I had contemplated modeling the depot for decades and had yet to devise a clear path forward. So I sort of tiptoed around the project by first kitbashing a Walthers interlocking tower kit into a surprisingly close

replica of the one that guarded the crossing. I was so enamored with the tower that I built it twice; the first time involved some compromises that came to haunt me.

I also had to build Thompson's grain elevator—a relatively easy kitbash of two Walthers kits—and the post office, another kitbash using a Pikestuff kit. The Fable House hotel behind the depot was dispatched in short order by using actual photos of the prototype reworked using the magic tools in Adobe's Photoshop Elements to replace the boarded-up windows and to remove recent tack-ons. Glued to a shell of .080" Evergreen styrene and with a 3-D styrene roof, porch, and windowsills, the photos did the job.

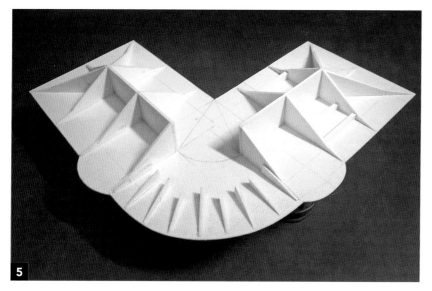

5

Left: The hip roof of the Cayuga depot is compound or cranked—it has two slopes. That means the 90-degree corner between the two wings comprises a pair of overlapping quarter conical sections. I made cardstock patterns to check my measurements before cutting .020" styrene cones. Other roof pieces are .080" styrene.

Below: I walked by this very scene countless times on my way into downtown Cayuga, Ind., from my home in the 1950s. So when the structures were installed and I happened to glance at them from this angle before calling it a night, I was startled by my strong reaction. It was like I was suddenly transported back to the '50s!

6

So there I was with nothing else to hide behind. It was time to build the depot.

One thing that experienced modelers learn is that you won't always clearly see the path forward. For example, the brick walls curved around the corner, and they formed half circles under each bay widow. Fortunately, brick sheets from N Scale Architect (they make HO stuff too) bonded to sheet styrene reduced this challenge to a workable project.

I got lucky when I discovered that a Tichy window molding was just the right size, when butted up to four compatriots, to create the five-windowed bays. Other Tichy windows and doors were deemed good enough for the tasks at hand.

Then came the roof. The depot had a hip roof—two of them, in fact, one per wing. The hip is cranked—that is, it starts with a shallow slope at the eaves, then segues to a much steeper slope up to the peak, **5**. At the corner of the two wings, the roof transitioned into a quarter circle where one steeply sloped quarter-cone truncated at the top fitted atop a shallow quarter-cone.

That done, I had to fabricate two full cones, one for each bay window, and fit them into the sloping roof. Cardstock templates and trial-and-error were the order of the day.

The most surprising aspect of the entire project occurred after I plunked the finished depot into its new home and stepped back to survey the scene: Shazam! I was instantly transported back to the '50s; I was back home again, **6**. I had somehow boarded a time machine and was back in the land of Elvis and blue suede shoes and pink Cadillacs and 45-rpm records.

A finer accolade to prototype modeling, I can't conceive.

1

CHAPTER EIGHT

An easier approach to prototype-based freelancing

A Chicago Great Western caboose from Centralia Car Shops (a special run of the Atlas NE-5 in all CGW paint schemes) trails a long freight on Jason Klocke's beautifully executed tribute to the CGW. Among other commercially painted HO CGW models were Athearn Genesis EMD Fs, Kato Alco RS-2s, and Stewart Baldwins and EMD Fs. *Jason Klocke*

Freelancing will remain as popular tomorrow as it is today and was yesterday. The need to freelance is quite another matter, however. The plethora of really well-detailed cars and locomotives and of railroad-specific laser-cut structure kits and now 3-D printing has made it easier than ever before to model a specific prototype, even one of the smaller railroads that used to be ignored by major manufacturers and importers, **1**. Many short lines, regional railroads, and Class 1s of modest proportions are now commercially supported in most popular scales.

Modeling a small railroad such as the Georgia Northeastern is appealing in that there's less to model and hence more time to focus on each element of the prototype (left). Tom Klimoski models the GNRR in HO scale (top), including the locomotive servicing facility in Tate, Ga. He scratchbuilt the distinctive sand tower using styrene.

2

Modest objectives

Tom Klimoski's Georgia Northeastern model railroad is what he calls "proto-freelanced." Many of the prototype industries on his layout are representations of the actual facilities that look close to what their full-size counterparts look like, but they are not exact models. "I took some liberties when designing my track plan," Tom recalled, "and I moved some of the industries closer together, omitted others, and rearranged the trackwork and sidings to accommodate the industries.

"The locomotive facility at Tate, however, **2**, is modeled after the prototype—a true Layout Design Element—so everyone who is familiar with it recognizes immediately," he continued. "And my model locomotive fleet now is pretty close to what the prototype Georgia Northeastern had in 2013, with the correct road numbers and EMD models, **3**. I guess you could say my layout is 'prototype inspired,' but it certainly is not 100 percent prototypical."

Tom's diesel fleet comprises five of the 10 units Georgia Northeastern had in 2013, the year he models. He custom painted the units after stripping the factory paint and lettered them with "a long-discontinued Microscale decal set (87-755) I have been able to find through friends and on eBay," Tom told me. "I was able to scrounge up enough sets to do my small fleet. I also added ditch lights

In both photos, the Georgia Northeastern units are crossing the Highway 53 grade crossing in Tate. Modeling even a simple grade-crossing scene becomes rewarding when the base proto-type is of modest length.
Prototype: D. Scott Chatfield; model: Tom Klimoski

3

and upgraded the decoders to ESU LokSound."

So while commercial support for Georgia Northeastern modelers is scant, with some effort even a little-known short line can be successfully modeled.

Cutting reasonable corners

Tom's approach suggests a reasonable, plausible path to prototype modeling. Nothing he has done, or not done, strays so far away from his base prototype to suggest he's doing

whatever happens to be convenient or "catch of the day."

Yet there are those among us, many in number, who cannot find the perfect prototype or who want to put their own personal stamp on their railroads. So what's the key to plausible freelancing?

Don't.

But since many of you are going to ignore that bit of advice, let me expand upon it a tad, hoping to reach the line of acceptability, a place where we can agree that we're on the same page. I'll

Old copies of the *Official Railway Equipment Register* can often be found at train shows and swap meets (right). Freight cars are listed by car number and car type under the owning railroad or private owner, making it easy to determine whether the Monon really did have a steel 40-foot boxcar numbered 1 (it did). In the back is a list of Association of American Railroad designations of car types such as XM for a standard boxcar, HM for a twin hopper, HT for a triple or quad hopper, LO for a covered hopper, and so on.

GULF, MOBILE AND OHIO RAILROAD CO.—CONTINUED.

FREIGHT EQUIPMENT Continued.

ITEM NUMBER	A.A.R. Mech. Designation	MARKINGS AND KIND OF CARS.	NUMBERS.	INSIDE Length	INSIDE Width	INSIDE Height	OUTSIDE LENGTH	OUTSIDE WIDTH At Eaves or Top of Sides or Platform	OUTSIDE WIDTH Extreme Width	HEIGHT FROM RAIL To Extreme Width	HEIGHT FROM RAIL To Eaves or Top of Sides or Platform	HEIGHT FROM RAIL To Top of Running Board	HEIGHT FROM RAIL To Extreme Height	DOORS SIDE Width of Open'g	DOORS SIDE Height of Open'g	DOORS END Width of Open'g	DOORS END Height of Open'g	CAPACITY Cubic Feet Level Full	CAPACITY Pounds or Gallons	Number of Cars
				ft. in.	ft. in.	ft. in.	ft. in.	ft. in.	ft. in.	ft. in.	ft. in.	ft. in.	ft. in.	ft. in.	ft. in.	ft. in.	ft. in.			
		Brought forward .... "G M & O"																		11471
1	XML	Box, All Steel....	59095 to 59097	50 6	9 2	10 5	51 10	9 10	10 5	5	13 11	15	15	9	10			4845	100000 lb.	3
2	XML	" All Steel, Hydro-frame Underframe	59200 to 59699	50 6	9 4	10 5	57 8	10	10 8	13 7	14	15	15	9				4932	140000 lb.	300
3	HM	Hopper, All Steel..	60000 to 60849	33	9 6	9 8	34	10 5	10 5	10 8	10 8		10 8					1970	100000 lb.	739
4	HM	" "	62000 to 62299	29 8	9 8	7 2	36	10 5	10 5	10 8	10 8		10 8					1629	190000 lb.	300
5	FM	Flat, Steel.	70000 to 70449	41 6	9		42 4	9	9 10	3 8	4		5 11						100000 lb.	267
6	FM	" "	70500 to 70749	41 6	9 3		43 3	9	10 6	3 6	3 6		5 11						100000 lb.	250
7	LF	Wood Rack, Steel.	71000 to 71449	38 9	9		42 4	9	9 10	3 4	4		12 9						100000 lb.	21
11	LP	" " "	71500 to 71528	42	8 9		45	8 9	10 9	8 11	3 10		11 6						100000 lb.	1
12	FM	Flat, Steel.......	72000 to 72149	53 6	9 3		54 3	10 6	10 6	3 6	3 6		3 6						100000 lb.	70
13	FMS	" " Note J	74000	48 6	9 3	5 6	54 3	8 5	10 6	3 6	3 6		9 1						100000 lb.	1
14	FMS	" " Note J	74001, 74002	48 6	10 6	8	54 3	8 5	10 6	3 6	3 6		11 6						100000 lb.	2
15	FMS	" " Note J	74050 to 74074	48 6	10 6	8 6	54 3	8 5	10 6	3 6	3 6		12						100000 lb.	25
16	FMS	" " Note J	★74075 to 74108	48 8	10 6	8 6	54 3	8 5	10 6	3 6	3 0		12						100000 lb.	34
17	FMS	" " Note J	74500	41	10 4	6	54 3	8 5	10 6	3 6	3 6		9 6						100000 lb.	1
21	FMS	" "	74525, 74526	49 6	10 6	8 6	54 3	8 5	10 6	3 6	3 6		12						100000 lb.	2
22	FMS	" " Note J	74600 to 74604	48 6	10 6	8 6	54 3	8 5	10 6	3 6	3 6		12						100000 lb.	5
23	FM	" "	75000 to 75019	41 6	9		42 4	9	9 10	3 8	4		5 11						100000 lb.	20
24	FD	" " Note D	79000	{57 9} {18 .}	9		58 4	9	10	3 3	{4 3} {2 .}		6 1						280000 lb.	1
25	LO	Covered Hopper.	80000 to 80149	29 3	9 5		35 3	10 1	10 7	8 5	11 9	12 10	13					1945	140000 lb.	150
26	LO	" "	80500 to 80649	29 3	9 5		35 3	10 1	10 7	8 5	11 9	12 10	13					1958	140000 lb.	145
31	LO	" "	80700 to 80749	41 1	9 11		47 1	10 8	10 8	8 6	12 8	13 3	13 3					3200	140000 lb.	50
32	LO	" "	80800 to 80899	41 1	9 5		47 1	10 5	10 1	12 2	12 5	13	13 11					2893	140000 lb.	100
33	LO	" "	80900 to 81024	41 1	9 11		47 1	10 8	10 8	3 6	12 8	13 3	13 3					3200	140000 lb.	75
34	HMS	Chip Hopper....	82000 to 82199	33	9 6	14 6	34	10 5	10 5	10 8	15 6		15 6					3436	100000 lb.	200
35	HMS	" "	82200 to 82343	33	9 5	12 3	34	10 8	13 7	15 6			15 6					3500	100000 lb.	144
36	HM	Hopper, All Steel	82500 to 82600	32	10 4	7 5	34	10 5	10 5	3 3	10 8		10 8					2191	100000 lb.	40
37	FM	Flat, Steel......	90500 to 90999	44 4	8 9		45	10 9	10 9	3 10	4 1		4 1						100000 lb.	16
41	XML	Box...Notes E, K	103000 to 103149	50 6	9 2	10 6	53	9 5	10 6		14 6	15 1	15 1	8	9 10			4872	100000 lb.	150
42	SM	Stock, S. D., Steel Underfrm. Note A	108000 to 108199	40 4	8 5	7 9	42 1	9 8	10 2	3 11	12 4	12 10	14 4	5	7 4			2631	80000 lb.	60
43	SF	Stock, D. D., Steel Underfrm. Note A	109000 to 109099	40 4	8 5	3 7	42 1	9 8	10 2	3 11	12 4	12 10	14 4	5	3 4				80000 lb.	15
		Total..																		14658

RECAPITULATION OF CAR EQUIPMENT.

Class X—Box Car Type.
AGGREGATE AND AVERAGE.

A.A.R. Mech. Desig.	Inside Length ft. in.	Number of Cars	Capacity Cubic Feet	Aggregate Capacity Cubic Feet	Marked Capacity (Pounds)
XM ..	40 6 ..	85 ..	3311 ..	281,435 ..	100,000
XM ..	40 6 ..	118 ..	3645 ..	430,110 ..	100,000
XM ..	40 6 ..	1,597 ..	3710 ..	5,924,870 ..	80,000
XM ..	40 6 ..	24 ..	3805 ..	91,320 ..	80,000
XM ..	40 6 ..	374 ..	3868 ..	1,444,632 ..	100,000
XM ..	40 6 ..	1,350 ..	3895 ..	5,263,305 ..	100,000

A.A.R. Mech. Desig.	Inside Length ft. in.	Number of Cars	Capacity Cubic Feet	Aggregate Capacity Cubic Feet	Marked Capacity (Pounds)
XM ..	40 6 ..	1,070 ..	3898 ..	4,170,860 ..	100,000
XM ..	40 6 ..	48 ..	3900 ..	187,200 ..	80,000
XM ..	40 6 ..	1,156 ..	3900 ..	4,508,400 ..	100,000
XM ..	50 6 ..	838 ..	4845 ..	4,060,110 ..	100,000
XM ..	50 6 ..	50 ..	4862 ..	243,100 ..	100,000
XM ..	50 6 ..	45 ..	4928 ..	221,760 ..	100,000
XM ..	50 6 ..	597 ..	4932 ..	2,944,404 ..	100,000
XML ..	40 6 ..	10 ..	3868 ..	38,680 ..	100,000
XML ..	40 6 ..	2 ..	3898 ..	7,796 ..	100,000

A.A.R. Mech. Desig.	Inside Length ft. in.	Number of Cars	Capacity Cubic Feet	Aggregate Capacity Cubic Feet	Marked Capacity (Pounds)
XML ..	40 6 ..	25 ..	3900 ..	97,500 ..	100,000
XML ..	50 6 ..	3 ..	4845 ..	14,535 ..	100,000
XML ..	50 6 ..	150 ..	4872 ..	730,800 ..	100,000
XML ..	50 6 ..	300 ..	4932 ..	1,479,600 ..	140,000
Total....		7,851		32,172,417	

Average cubical capacity per car (for Commodity Loading)...4098

Plain Box (XM)—
Cars of 80,000 lbs. capacity.. 1,669
Cars of 100,000 lbs. " .. 5,692

Box (XML)—
Cars of 100,000 lbs. capacity.. 190
Cars of 140,000 lbs. " .. 300

TOTAL BOX CARS (Includes all class X cars)......... 7,851

Class S—Stock Car Type.

A.A.R. Mech. Desig.	Inside Length ft. in.	Number of Cars	Capacity (Pounds)
SM	40 4	60	80,000
SF	40 4	15	80,000
Total........		75	

Class G—Gondola Car Type.

A.A.R. Mech. Desig.	Inside Length ft. in.	Number of Cars	Capacity Cubic Feet	Marked Capacity (Pounds)
GB ..	41 3 ..	718 ..	1825 ..	100,000
GB ..	41 6 ..	18 ..	1825 ..	100,000
GB ..	41 6 ..	670 ..	1840 ..	100,000
GB ..	41 6 ..	19 ..	1896 ..	100,000
GB ..	65 5 ..	75 ..	1777 ..	140,000
GB ..	65 6 ..	25 ..	1777 ..	140,000

A.A.R. Mech. Desig.	Inside Length ft. in.	Number of Cars	Capacity Cubic Feet	Capacity (Pounds)
GBR ..	41 6 ..	20 ..	1840 ..	100,000
GBSR ..	41 6 ..	5 ..	1810 ..	100,000
GS ..	41 6 ..	223 ..	1825 ..	100,000
GS ..	41 6 ..	227 ..	1896 ..	100,000
Total...		2,000		

Gondola, Solid Bottom (GB)—
Cars of 100,000 lbs. capacity.. 1,425
Cars of 140,000 lbs " " .. 100

Gondola, Roofed (GBR, GBSR)—
Cars of 100,000 lbs. capacity.. 25

Gondola, Dump outside of rails (GS)—
Cars of 100,000 lbs. capacity.. 450
Total................. 2,000

Class F—Flat Car Type.

A.A.R. Mech. Desig.	Inside Length ft. in.	Number of Cars	Marked Capacity (Pounds)
FB ..	57 9 ..	1 ..	280,000
FM ..	41 6 ..	537 ..	100,000
FM ..	44 4 ..	16 ..	100,000
FM ..	53 6 ..	70 ..	100,000
FMS ..	41 ..	1 ..	100,000
FMS ..	48 6 ..	33 ..	100,000
FMS ..	48 8 ..	34 ..	100,000
FMS ..	49 6 ..	2 ..	100,000
Total........		694	

Flat (All Class F cars except FB and FL)—
Cars of 100,000 lbs. capacity.. 693
Cars of 280,000 lbs. capacity.. 1
Total..................... 694

Note A—Bills for repairs to G. M. & O. box cars in series 7500 to 7524 and stock cars in series 108000 to 108199 and 109000 to 109099 and reports of cars damaged or destroyed or requests for material needed for repairs should be sent to H. M. Nelson, Vice Pres. & Chief Mech. Officer, North American Car Corporation, 77 So. Wacker Drive, Chicago 6, Ill.

Note C—Cars in series 48050 to 48054 are equipped with roofs and bulkheads.

Note D—Dimensions of depressed section of car No. 79000 are as follows: length 18 ft., width 9 ft., height from top of rail to top of platform 2 ft. This car is equipped with steel loading floor and has 2 six-wheel trucks. Spacing between truck centers 40 ft., between axles 5 ft.

Note E—Bills for repairs to G.M.& O. box cars in series 103000 to 103149 should be sent to V. C. McMullen, Chief Maintenance Officer, General American Transportation Corp., P. O. Box 480, East Chicago, Ind.

Note F—Cars in series 1425 to 1499 are equipped with fork lift truck pallets, platforms or skids, which will be considered part of the car.

Note H—Cars in series 59000 to 59050 are equipped with 19 DF Belt Rails and cross bars for special loading.

Note J—Cars in series 74000 to 74002, 74050 to 74074, 74075 to 74108, 74500 and 74600 to 74604 are equipped with permanent bulkheads; suitable for transporting wall-board.

Note K—Cars in series 103000 to 103149 are equipped with "DF" loading equipment having 8 belt rails.

★ Denotes additions. ◆ Denotes increase. ▮ Denotes reduction. (See Page xviii.)

Compare the Boston & Maine EMD F2 (left, on Jim Dufour's HO railroad at Troy Ledges, N.H.) and Lehigh Valley Alco FA (top right) paint schemes. At first glance, the stripe colors make them look different, but the graphics are right out of the EMD stylebook. A different body color and B&M or LV decals create a new but plausible freelanced paint scheme. Jack Ozanich and Craig Wilson took a similar approach as shown on a set of Atlantic Great Eastern F3s passing Karas' General Store at Center Monson, Maine (bottom right). AGE diesels follow LV practices, such as the cab-side walkway for access to the windshield, and paint scheme (using Microscale LV decal striping) except the bottom stripe is wider and the red is a bit brighter than LV Cornell Red. *B&M: Jim Dufour; LV: Rich Taylor; AGE: Craig Wilson*

then extrapolate on the meaning of "don't" to include "don't push it any further than you have to." I'll also point out that I qualified "freelancing" with "plausible." And I'll add that you're reading a book that proposes to apply lessons from the prototype, so presumably we are all interested in adhering to prototype practices to a reasonable degree.

For the purposes of this particular discussion, we're therefore assuming that your goal is not to have a railroad that is just a small assemblage of tracks and rolling stock and structures and scenery with virtually no ties to full-size railroading. Those who seek to build such railroads have very personal goals, and it's almost impossible to offer them constructive advice. They

know better than anyone what their goals are.

But for those of you who aspire to the creation of a railroad that, had it been constructed to 12-inch-to-the-foot scale, might actually have eked out a living in the North American rail network—that is, to embrace a plausible theme—while not making your life miserable in the process, there are some things you can do to make your task a lot easier while making your railroad a lot more realistic. Looking to a base prototype is a good start.

Why look to a base prototype or prototypes? It's just easier that way. You can capitalize on things the big guys did that you admire while ignoring those that don't quite suit

your needs or tastes. And you can borrow everything from paint schemes to route maps.

I got an email from someone who is freelancing a medium-size Appalachian coal road along the lines of the Virginian, Clinchfield, or Western Maryland—not a big-time outfit like the Norfolk & Western, Baltimore & Ohio, Chesapeake & Ohio, or Louisville & Nashville. He's modeling 1969–70 and wondered whether it would be appropriate to run fleets of 55- and 70-ton hoppers along with some 100 tonners.

I remembered seeing a number of "steam-era" hoppers in a Chessie freight rolling through Williamsburg, Va., when daughter Sue was in college there, which was 1983–87 (yes, I had

The Nickel Plate Road's Alco PA-1s were dubbed Bluebirds for obvious reasons. The paint scheme is an Alco design; EMD graphic designers would never have stair-stepped the road name down the side of the carbody. Using Photoshop Elements' "Replace Color" tool, you can experiment with ways to adjust a factory paint scheme to reflect personal tastes for a prototype-based freelanced railroad without venturing too far away from plausibility.

6

7

These Durham & Southern Baldwin road switchers wear a typical Baldwin paint scheme. Baldwin designers often employed narrow or wide stripes ending in half circles, but they were usually asked to adapt EMD paint schemes.

8

Back in the 1970s, I striped this Atlas RSD-4 using Herald King EMD Geep decals, which are not correctly proportioned for Alco units. Today, I would use a factory-painted Athearn (former Model Die Casting/Roundhouse) or Atlas Nickel Plate Road model and simply apply Midland Road road-name decals and a new road number.

to ask my wife). So in his era, smaller twin and triple hoppers are fine.

But a better answer was to recommend that he check the websites of various railroad historical societies to find both locomotive and freight car rosters for railroads similar to his freelanced line. And at a swap meet or on eBay, he might find a 1969 copy of the *Official Railway Equipment Register*, **4**, which lists each railroad's cars by type and number and includes enough basic dimensional data for you to figure out what type of hopper or boxcar or covered hopper they're referring to.

This applies to locomotives as well, although there is no convenient official register for them. Thanks to books and magazine articles and websites, however, it's but an evening's work to check the roster of a few favorite railroads to see what types of units they operated in key years. Plagiarizing their locomotive rosters should be a primary goal.

That's what I meant by "don't." Don't reinvent the wheel. Don't make up a roster based on what you happen to have randomly acquired over the years. Don't run one of these and one of those when a half-dozen of each of a few locomotive types will create a much more plausible roster.

Yes, there are exceptions to every rule, and you can find railroads, especially short lines, that did indeed roster one of these and two of those. They're typically "previously owned" power from connecting railroads. But that leads me to the last don't: Don't model the exceptional if your goal is plausibility. Having to wave your hands as you explain away your railroad's shortcomings or eccentricities is not a becoming trait.

Back in 1995, I coined the term "Layout Design Element" to describe the age-old practice of modeling actual locations. This is especially important for freelancers, as very few of them have enough knowledge to design towns and yards and engine terminals that look familiar (plausible) and function realistically.

The same thing applies to car and locomotive rosters: Look to the prototype. When plausibility is the objective, the answers lie there.

Paint schemes

If you're modeling first-generation diesels, you can be sure that one of a very few graphic designers created the livery for your fleet of locomotives. That's why so many of the products of General Motors' Electro-Motive Division have similar graphics, **5**. And EMD paint schemes migrated to Alco and Baldwin in subsequent orders, often with less satisfactory results.

Alco, **6**, and Baldwin, **7**, did originate some remarkable designs of their own. If your freelanced paint scheme doesn't reflect such designs, it is likely to stand out as an imposter. The more creative you are, the less plausible your paint scheme is likely to be.

The good news is that you can save time, effort, and even money by adapting commercial decal sets or factory paint schemes. Change one color or perhaps scrub off the original road name and add your own custom decals, **8**, and your prototype-based freelanced roster is ready for action.

"Family" paint schemes

If you've never seen a New England Central locomotive before, the one

9

10

In the late 1950s, the Nickel Plate apparently decided that the expense associated with the multi-stripe scheme, as shown on GP9 528, wasn't worth the extra cost and specified a simplified scheme with a richer yellow, worn by repainted GP9 462 in Lafayette, Ind., in April 1966. It was probably more visible to motorists at grade crossings too.

New England Central's daily wood chip train, powered by an ex-Canadian National GP40-2W in Genesee & Wyoming family colors, crosses the Lamoille River at East Georgia, Vt. (top). Changing the initials on the herald in effect creates a plausible new paint scheme, as Richard Deuso has done on his Franklin & Lamoille Railroad, shown by GE U23B 2201 crossing the Connecticut River bridge (right). *Two photos: Richard Deuso*

shown in photo **9** may nevertheless look somewhat familiar because of its orange-and-black paint scheme. That livery is shared among all of the railroads in the Genesee & Wyoming family. A closer look at a number of G&W-family locomotives would show that only the initials on the herald change from railroad to railroad.

This offers advantages for model railroaders who aspire to model a modern short line or regional railroad. First, G&W-family locomotives often move between properties, especially as new railroads are acquired. So you could operate a mix of G&W-owned and -painted locomotives along with as-yet unpainted locomotives of the

acquired railroad. And, with some care, it's usually practical to buy a factory-painted unit and simply add custom decals for the new herald.

Photographer Richard Deuso has done just that, in fact. His freelanced Franklin & Lamoille RR, which operates over the former St. Johnsbury & Lamoille County RR, has adopted

11

the standard G&W livery. Anyone familiar with modern shortline and regional railroading will recognize the paint scheme and bestow instant credibility on Richard's mythical but plausible railroad.

An earlier example of a paint scheme used by multiple railroads under a single ownership blanket was the Salzberg lines. Among them was the Unadilla Valley, which Iain Rice described in *Model Railroad Planning* 2014. Their fleet of GE 70-tonners in an orange and cream paint scheme was familiar to shortline fans and modelers.

Showing change over time

Like everything else, railroads evolve. This is most obvious as they acquire new motive power or types of rolling stock, but it also shows as paint

schemes are revised, often in an effort to save money but perhaps to show the imprint of new management.

The freelancer is too often content with creating a "now" paint scheme and calling it quits. If he or she is modeling first- or even second-generation diesels and has done a good job, likely as not the livery will reflect the near-standard designs of one of the Big Three builders: Alco, Electro-Motive, or General Electric.

But when those units came due for a refresh, or when new units were ordered, the powers that be may have dictated a simpler scheme to save shop time: two colors instead of three, less masking of stripes, or whatever, **10**.

Prototype-based freelanced railroads should also show the passage of time in both obvious and more subtle ways.

Jack Ozanich's Atlantic Great Eastern, one of the most skillfully executed proto-freelanced model railroads, abounds with clues as to its heritage. For example, some AGE paint schemes go back nearly 40 years; some warhorse Atlas units were in service on Jack's previous layout in Paw Paw, Mich.

The AGE is jointly controlled and equipment influenced by the Lehigh Valley (diesel locomotives), Canadian National (steam locomotives), and Canadian Pacific (cabooses). I'll let official AGE photographer Craig Wilson carry on the narrative:

"When we obtained a Walthers EMD SW1 years ago, I drew up several potential paint schemes for it. The SW1s were the first diesels purchased in the 1940s, so one of the schemes I drew was for the 1940s steam-

Rosters of prototype-based freelanced railroads should also show the passage of time in subtle as well as obvious ways. These three switchers on Jack Ozanich's superbly executed Atlantic Great Eastern show how the diesel paint scheme evolved from the steam-inspired 1940s black scheme on SW1 193 at right to the first red scheme on Alco S-2 227 at left to the current wider-stripe scheme in the EMD SW1200RS 330 at center. *Craig Wilson*

locomotive-inspired scheme on AGE 193, **11**. It uses the large AGE herald like on the steam locomotive tenders and the cab numbers are from the same Champion decal set used on the steamers.

"AGE 227 is an Alco S-2. This was the yard-lead engine this day and is sitting 'on spot' across from the South Dover yard office. This Atlas unit wears the first red scheme, which was adopted with the purchase of the Alco RS-1 road switchers in the early 1950s.

"AGE 330 is an EMD SW1200RS. The 1960 purchase of EMD GP18s and a pair of SW1200RSs spelled the end of steam. These locomotives

introduced a new look with a wider black stripe on the hoods and white/ black chevrons on the nose. AGE 330 has extra flags mounted, indicating that it has been readied for a transfer run or perhaps an extra bound for the Clayton Lake subdivision."

Anyone who has doubts about prototype-based freelancing being a form of prototype modeling need only to look to the Atlantic Great Eastern for affirmation.

Going back to Richard Deuso's photo, **9**, the big clock on the wall showing the passage of long periods of time is the bridge. The girders show rust, and some of that has cascaded

down the concrete piers. The steel cutwater on the upstream side of the center pier is also badly rusted, and the concrete itself is chipped.

What turns the clock way back, however, is the stonework below the concrete pier extensions. The neatly cut and stacked stones have been encased in concrete at the base for added protection against winter ice and spring floods.

Give some thought to ways that your model railroad can or should show the passage and ravages of time. After all, even though you may have built it last year, it really wasn't "built" last year.

1

CHAPTER NINE

Correcting misimpressions

There are some closely held "truths" that no amount of well-intended correcting will ever stamp out. The problem is that they're based on facts that are correct as far as they go, but they are only half true in a larger context. A good example is the age-old debate about whether the piece of trackwork that allows a train to change routes is called a switch or a turnout, **1**. This device is actually both, and both terms are correct when properly used. The turnout is the whole shebang, whereas the switch is that part of the turnout that moves from side to side. So you can't "throw a turnout," and you can't have a "no. 8 switch."

Is this a switch or a turnout? It's actually both: The whole assembly is the turnout, and the part that moves is the switch. So you line or throw the switch, and you spike down a no. 8 turnout. The turnout number is a measure of the rail spread away from the frog; a number 8 means the rails have spread 1 foot apart when measured 8 feet from the point of the frog. The lower the frog number, the sharper the angle of divergence. In North America, both routes through the frog are straight; there are no "left-hand" or "right-hand" frogs.

Professional railroaders often scoff at modelers for using the term "turnout," which is understandable. They don't deal with turnouts; they throw switches—the part that moves. But railroad engineering drawings are clearly labeled "No. 10 Turnout," **2**, or whatever, not "No. 10 Switch." Simple as that.

But you can bet this debate will rage on for decades.

It ain't that hard!

With timetable and train-order (TTTO) operation becoming ever more popular, I am already hearing cries of alarm from those who have yet to experience it. We humans abhor change, and learning a seemingly complex system certainly embraces change. We fear that the hard-won knowledge of our past will not be relevant in this new arena. (I have yet to tap into most of the features of my ancient iPhone5, let alone buy one of the new ones!)

I subscribe to a chat group that comprises modelers who follow specific prototypes or base their freelanced railroads on one or more prototypes: prototype-based freelancing, which we chatted about in Chapter 6. Several of them model interesting short lines or regional railroads that can be operated alone or with one or two operators. For those who live in sparsely settled areas,

that is a plus. For those who don't want to do at home what they do for a living—manage people—a railroad of limited scope is just what the doctor ordered.

But it quickly became clear that some of them not only embrace their brand of railroading but have grave concerns about what it takes to model a busy mainline railroad and—horrors!—to cope with the arcane methodology of timetable and train-order railroading. Some British participants in the chat group made it clear that railway management on their side of the Atlantic would never have put up with such shenanigans.

Their concerns are well grounded in history. Back in railroading's formative years, unscheduled trains were not ordered to "run extra" but rather to "run wild." Indeed!

As the proud owner of a model railroad in which a few trains are told to, in effect, "run wild," let me assure the skeptics that their fears are misplaced. Yes, there are layouts where everything must operate on a precise schedule timed to the second, like Swiss railroads routinely do, thus putting a lot of pressure on the participants.

But that's not the norm and certainly not the goal for most of us. The objective is to re-create what happened on the full-size railroads in a given time and place. Railroaders tell me that even the Nickel Plate Road's vaunted "High Speed Service" reputation didn't preclude trains from running late. Retired NKP engineer Don Daily recommended that I start the 3:1 clock, **3**, before I hold my pre-session crew briefing to ensure that trains start late. "By the time westbounds got from New York to western Indiana, you can bet they were an hour or more behind schedule," he coached me.

My point is it's very easy to assume that, once a clock starts to unwind and someone hands you a schedule, your fate is sealed: Measure up or face the consequences. That may be true for Long Island Rail Road commuter trains or today's hot UPS trains, but it didn't apply to the day-to-day business

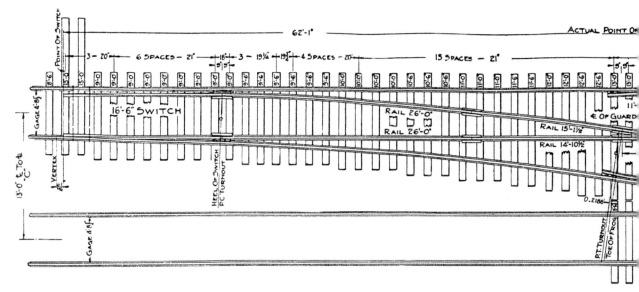

TYPICAL LAYOUT OF Nº 7 CROSSOVER

OFFSET DIAGRAM

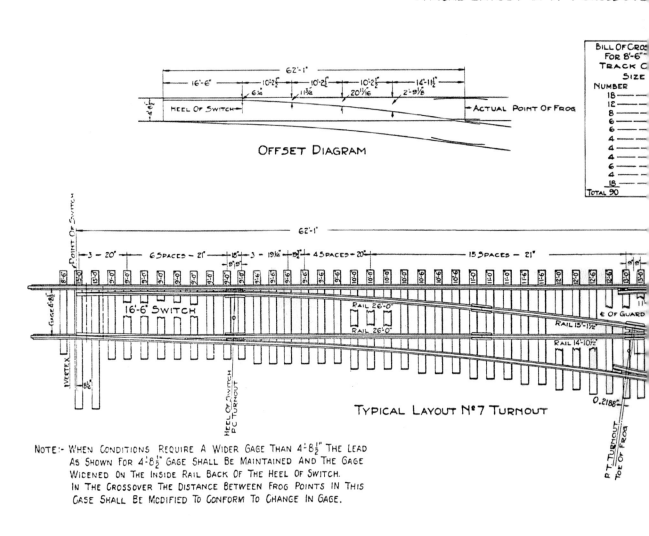

TYPICAL LAYOUT Nº 7 TURNOUT

NOTE:- WHEN CONDITIONS REQUIRE A WIDER GAGE THAN 4'-8½" THE LEAD
AS SHOWN FOR 4'-8½" GAGE SHALL BE MAINTAINED AND THE GAGE
WIDENED ON THE INSIDE RAIL BACK OF THE HEEL OF SWITCH.
IN THE CROSSOVER THE DISTANCE BETWEEN FROG POINTS IN THIS
CASE SHALL BE MODIFIED TO CONFORM TO CHANGE IN GAGE.

2

Railroad engineering drawings for turnouts are clearly labeled as such, not as "No. 7 Switches," for example. Professional railroaders deal only with the moving part of the turnout called the switch. In turn, modelers misuse the word turnout, as in

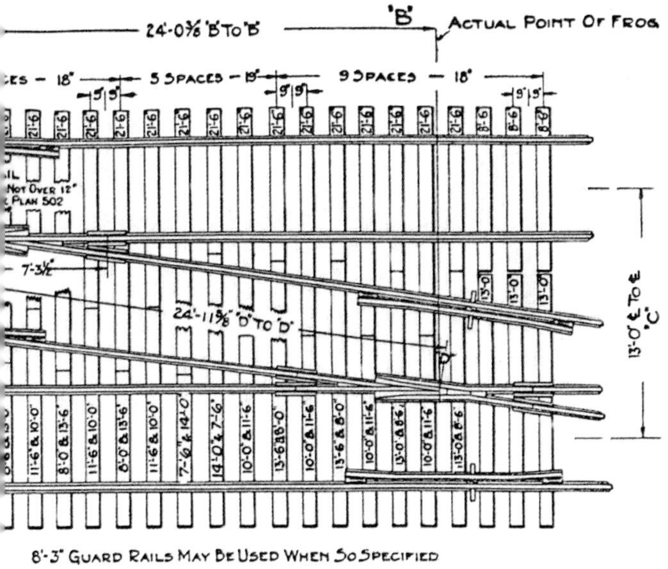
24'-0⅞" 'B' To 'B'
'B'
Actual Point Of Frog
5 Spaces – 18"
9 Spaces – 18"
24'-11⅝" 'D' To 'D'
13'-0" ℄ To ℄ 'C'
8'-3" Guard Rails May Be Used When So Specified

Table Of Track Centers	
Distance 'C' ℄ To ℄	Distance 'B' 'B' Bet. Act. Frog Pts.
11'-0"	10'-1¼"
11'-6"	13'-7⅛"
12'-0"	17'-0⅞"
12'-6"	20'-6⅝"
13'-0"	24'-0⅞"
13'-6"	27'-6¼"
14'-0"	31'-0"
14'-6"	34'-5¾"
15'-0"	37'-11⅝"
15'-6"	41'-5⅜"
16'-0"	44'-11⅛"

Change Of 1 Foot In Distance 'C' Changes Distance 'B' 'B'-6'-11⅝.

Table Of Track Centers	
Distance 'C' ℄ To ℄	Distance 'D' 'D' Bet. Act Frog Pts
11'-0"	10'-10¾"
11'-6"	14'-5"
12'-0"	17'-11⅛"
12'-6"	21'-5⅜"
13'-0"	24'-11⅝"
13'-6"	28'-5¾"
14'-0"	32'-0"
14'-6"	35'-6¼"
15'-0"	39'-0½"
15'-6"	42'-6⅝"
16'-0"	46'-0⅞"

Change Of 1 Foot In Distance 'C' Changes Distance 'D' 'D'-7'-0½.

Bill Of Crossover Ties For 8'-6" Track Ties Track Centers 13'-0" Size 7"x 9"
Substituting For The 21'-6" Timbers Shorter Lengths As Indicated.

Number	Length
2	7'-6"
4	8'-0"
4	8'-6"
18	9'-0"
12	9'-6"
16	10'-0"
6	10'-6"
6	11'-0"
12	11'-6"
4	12'-0"
4	12'-6"
10	13'-0"
4	13'-6"
2	14'-0"
4	15'-0"
Total 108	B.M. 6059 FT

Bill Of Turnout Ties For 8'-6" Track Ties Size 7"x9"

Number	Length
9	9'-0"
6	9'-6"
4	10'-0"
3	10'-6"
3	11'-0"
2	11'-6"
2	12'-0"
2	12'-6"
3	13'-0"
2	13'-6"
2	14'-0"
2	14'-6"
4	15'-0"
2	15'-6"
2	16'-0"
3	16'-6"
Total 51	B.M. 3203 Ft.

NOTE: If 8'-0" Track Ties Are Used Deduct 6" From Length Of Ties Given In Table, Except The 2-15'-0" Head Block Ties Total Number 48 B.M. 2822 Ft.

Actual Point Of Frog.

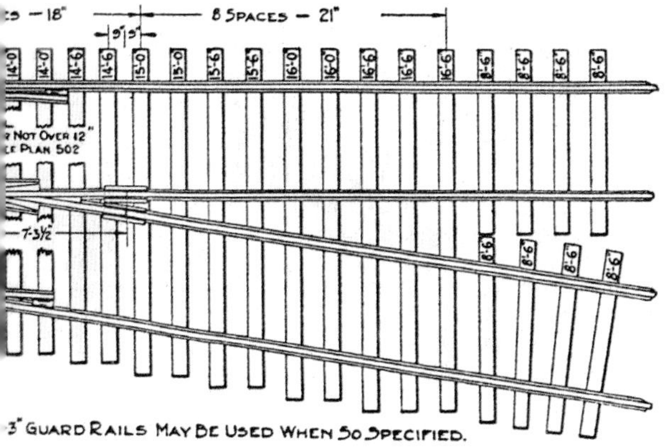
8 Spaces – 21"
3" Guard Rails May Be Used When So Specified.

Data

Frog Nº	7
Frog Angle	8°10'-16"
Frog Length	12'-0"
Length Of Switch Points	16'-6"
Heel Spread Of Switch	6¼"
Switch Angle	1°44'-11"
Lead	62'-1"
Radius Of Curve	361.69'
Degree Of Curve	15°53'-30"
Central Angle Of Curve	6°26'-05"
Straight Closure	40'-10½"
Curved Closure	41'-1½"

A. R. E. A.
LAYOUT
NO. 7 TURNOUT & CROSSOVER

SEPTEMBER, 15, 1919.
REVISED SEPT. 20, 1920.

PLAN NO. 902

Adopted March, 1921 Revised, 1929

"throw the turnout." This (pre-AAR) American Railways Association drawing clearly defines the whole assembly as a no. 7 turnout; the hinged 16'-6" switch is also clearly marked.

Ideally, fast clocks are not used as a means of forcing adherence to schedules but rather as a tool to judge how related events are unfolding. If everything moved per the published schedule, train orders would not have been invented. Back when my "scenery" comprised a few structures, 3:1 fast clocks mounted around the railroad room were already fully functional. Nothing encourages progress on a layout like regular operating sessions.

of running most freight trains. A timetable schedule is a 12-hour-wide window of opportunity to move a train, not a minute-by-minute account of its expected progress.

Rest assured that none of the experienced layout owners I routinely operate with see the movement of trains and cars as some sort of high-stakes game. It's a simulation; they view their railroads as enterprises that make business decisions intended to serve their customers in a safe and efficient manner. That the trains are only a small percentage of the size of their prototypes isn't on anyone's radar screen. The goal is to model railroading as it was or is—and to have a lot of fun doing it, **4**.

Everything's relative

It was January 1988 and well below zero in New Hampshire, where son John attended college. His basketball team (did I mention he stands 6'-7"?)

managed to escape winter's icy grip by playing games in Florida, where it was sunny and 69 degrees.

"We all immediately donned shorts and T-shirts," John recalls. "There were five or six guys at the pool with no shirts, and three of them jumped into the outdoor pool.

"A New Jersey high school buddy, Marty, came over to the hotel to say hello. He was wearing a long-sleeve shirt and a hooded jacket, and he was cold. When he saw the guys jumping in the pool, I thought his eyes were going to pop out of his head. I told him he'd been in Florida too long!"

Everything's relative.

When I originally wrote this, several weeks of single-digit temperatures had just departed, and I could actually see grass instead of snow in my front yard for the first time in more than a month. The temperature peaked at 55 degrees that day, and I went out to get the papers and mail in

a golf shirt. Nice warm day, I thought.

But last fall when the temperature dropped to 55, I was downright chilly.

Everything's relative.

The debate about which scale and gauge are The Best has raged since scales were numbered Naught, One, Two, and so on. Naught is printed 0, which looks odd, so it became O, and a scale about half its size became H-O, now HO.

The "tiny" scale, O, seemed a bit puny compared to No. 1 gauge trains—still does, in fact. You see No. 1 gauge stuff all the time, as that's the gauge used for 1:32 "large scale" standard-gauge models. Bulked-up 1:29 models also roll on No. 1 gauge track, as do LGB's 1:22.5 G scale meter-gauge (technically, Gnm) trains and Bachmann's 1:20.3 Fn3 trains.

No matter the technicalities; anyone can see that large scale is, well, larger than O scale, which is about twice the size and eight times the bulk of HO.

4 Jim Leighty (left) and Mike Quinn are focused on their work as the crew of westbound local No. 45 switching Cayuga, Ind. But since they will have to use the main line for switching, they also have to know what time it is and whether any superior trains are due, and they have to flag against westbound extra trains, which could arrive at any time.

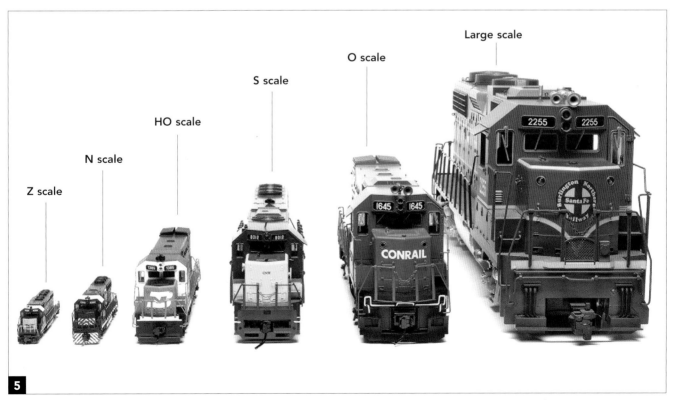

5 It's easy to judge which locomotive is "big" and which is "little." Or is it? Doesn't one's perception of size depend on previous experiences? Over time, we become accustomed to whatever scale we work in. *Bill Zuback*

6

Between O and HO is S scale at 1:64. And below HO is TT scale, at 1:120. It still has some following in Europe and a few holdouts on this side of the Atlantic. It's not hard to understand why: In a more logical world, we probably could have gotten by quite nicely with S and TT alone, but that's not how the cards were played.

Then along came OOO, later standardized in North America at 1:160 and called N scale. Predictably, it was just over half as large as HO. The downward progression continued,

perhaps to prove it could be done, with Z scale at 1:220, **5**. There are some remarkably well-detailed and good-running models in that scale, and anyone who dismisses it out of hand not only has a short memory about how we viewed N scale in its formative years but also hasn't paid attention to the wonderful products from American Z Line and Micro-Trains.

There is no ideal scale, nor is there a wrong scale. What works for one person may not fit the needs of another. Put more positively, today one may enjoy modeling—not just

running little trains in circles but prototype modeling—in a wide variety of scales and gauges. He or she may, for example, model long double-stack freights in N scale in the basement, have a large-scale garden railroad out back, and enjoy puttering around with an On3 or Sn3 logging railroad in a spare room. Imperialism in model railroading knows no bounds.

A fascinating thing about the various scales is how their apparent size changes depending on how we compare them. I have operated on several N scale layouts, and after an

If O scale seems too large, perhaps it's not the scale but the scope that is the problem. Modeling a short line or a rural branch of a major railroad such as one of the Wabash lines that hosted their classic Moguls might be just the ticket. Here Wabash 2-6-0 No. 573 steams through Timewell, Ill., on a chartered trip that nonetheless shows the modeling potential of simple scenes and short trains. Kemtron made an O scale brass craftsman kit that can occasionally be found assembled at swap meets, but any light steam power or small diesel would be a worthy pinch hitter. *Ed Wilkommen; courtesy Paul Swanson, Lake States Archives, photo 2018.15.N94.7755*

hour or so, their size seemed "normal." When I got home, my HO models were suddenly transformed into massive beasts. The cure for that is to stop by Tom Piccirillo's O scale traction layout or take a ride behind his live steam locomotive; HO soon becomes rather compact once again!

Physical limitations may point us toward a certain scale and gauge. For example, aging eyes make O or larger scale models appealing, as do less-steady hands. It's nice to be able to see what we're trying to accomplish and then what we actually did accomplish.

Infirmities aside, I recommend walking a mile in another modeler's shoes before you decide that your age-old favorite scale has lost some of its luster. It could be that you simply need a refresher course in its advantages. Drop by a friend's or a club's layout that features a different scale, and then take another look at your current models with "fresh eyes"—as though you had never seen them before. You may rediscover the attributes that attracted you to them in the first place.

And, in line with the premise of this book, consider what's available

in each scale as that relates to your modeling objectives. HO isn't the most popular scale by a sizable margin simply because of its size. The wide array of products makes it easier to model a specific prototype in 1:87 than in any other scale. And O scale isn't large if your modeling objectives aren't vast; consider a Wabash branch line powered by a classic Mogul, **6**, or an Iowa interurban playing its last cards.

Misimpressions are easier to develop than they are to lay aside. Be sure yours aren't preventing you from attaining your modeling objectives.

1

CHAPTER TEN

Towns by the names and numbers

One of the very first concerns facing a yardmaster tasked with blocking freight cars in station

order, thus making it easier for switch crews to do their work at each town, is the sequence

of towns. Do cars for Linden get blocked before or after those for Cayuga, **1**? We can't

expect our friends who operate our railroads perhaps once a month to remember such arcane

information. Our professional colleagues did this day in and day out, so they pretty much had

the order of things nailed down by rote. But even they employed tricks of the trade.

There are a lot of cars in the NKP's westbound yard at Frankfort, Ind., and only some of those, called "shorts," are destined for locals. And only some of those are destined for No. 45, the KC Local, which serves the modeled Third Subdivision of the St. Louis Division. Each car has to be blocked in station (numerical) order to make switching the towns easier for the local's crew.

When I first had the opportunity to operate on Allen McClelland's original Virginian & Ohio layout in the early 1970s, I was eager to make a good impression. But I had almost zero experience operating on a railroad as sophisticated as the V&O.

Fortunately, Allen had devised a simple way for "boomers" (visiting crews), as well as his regulars, to remember the sequence of towns: He named them in alphabetical order: Afton, Blackstone, Clintwood, Dawson Spring, Elm Grove, Fullerton, Gage Pass, Highland Wye, Indian Hill, and Jimtown. I can remember them this to this day.

Professional railroaders often used a similar and equally simple means of keeping track of what went where. Rather than asking the townsfolk of the villages the railroad passed through for permission to rename them in alphabetical order—and what would they have done if there were more than 26 towns on a division?—they used another handy device: station numbers.

I first heard of this from retired Illinois Central conductor Chet French, who told me they blocked cars in station-number order on the line he worked. Decades later, I employ a similar, and prototypical, system to aid yardmasters and local-freight crews as they strive to sort cars into the proper order.

The New York, Chicago & St. Louis, better known as the Nickel Plate Road, added to its route miles in the early 1920s by absorbing the former Lake Erie & Western and the Toledo, St. Louis & Western ("Clover Leaf") railroads. To avoid confusion when using milepost numbers for station identification, they appended a 1 to the mileposts of former LE&W lines and a 2 to those on the Clover Leaf. So station 266 on the Clover Leaf, my former hometown of Cayuga, Ind., became 2266, **2**.

Switching cars into the desired sequence for the four locals that depart the classification hub at Frankfort, Ind., each day thus became a simple matter of sorting waybills, and hence cars, by station order. Since milepost numbers increase in the westerly direction on my modeled Third Subdivision, cars for the westbound KC Local (second-class train No. 45) that have waybills with the lowest station numbers are blocked right behind the locomotive. Those with the highest numbers are next to the caboose.

This requires that I include station numbers on waybills. I decided to list station numbers only on those waybills for "shorts"—that is, cars that are destined for towns short of the next division point, and hence usually switched into local freights. When a yardmaster, **3**, sees a station number on a waybill, he knows that this car goes on a local. The name of the division and town precedes the station number, so he knows which division's local should get that car. (Of the four divisions radiating out of Frankfort, one—the Third Sub of the St. Louis Division—is modeled and three are staged, but all four locals are blocked.)

When the Frankfort yardmaster receives a waybill for a car routed NKP-ST. LOUIS DIV.-CAYUGA (2266), he can tell at a glance that the car is headed down the St. Louis Division to the modeled town of Cayuga (station number 2266). He therefore blocks it behind cars with 2000-series numbers less than 2266 and ahead of cars with numbers higher than 2266.

The particular car shown in **2** had a carload of cement from Tennessee headed for Jenkins Cement in Cayuga.

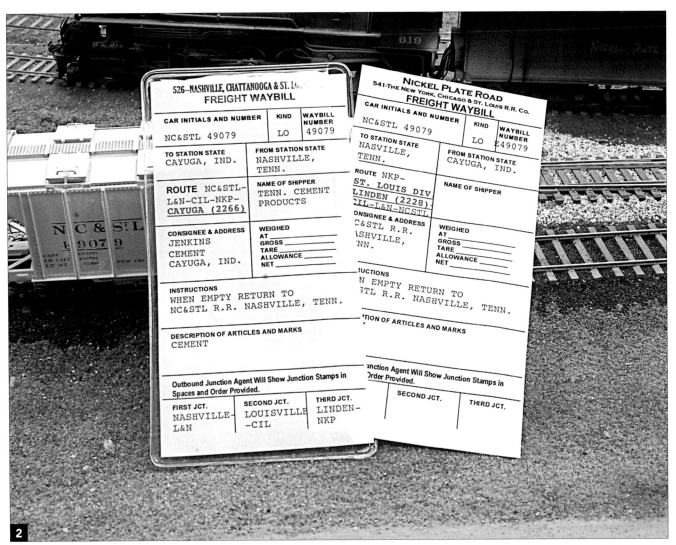

2

This waybill shows at a glance the routing, which includes the division name and—for cars to be delivered on the layout—the town and related station number of the car's consignee. This Nashville, Chattanooga & St. Louis covered hopper (AAR type LO) arrived on the NKP from the Monon at Linden, Ind., and was delivered to Jenkins Cement at Cayuga (station 2266). It's now empty and will be sent back home via the reverse route by moving an already prepared empty waybill from the bottom of the "deck" in the clear-plastic sleeve to the top. In a few sessions (months), it will be back at Jenkins again.

When the local arrives in Cayuga, the crew can consult a track schematic, **2-6**, that shows which track that car should be spotted on. They can then put the waybill (facing the fascia to show its cycle has been fulfilled) into the bill box for Jenkins Cement.

Those of us who enjoy realistic operation have intense discussions concerning how much information to include on waybills or switch lists. The concern is that too much "noise" will cause the user's brain to generate a dial-tone sound as his or her eyes glaze over.

My view is that those who base our modeling on prototype practices should continue to push farther into authentic operating procedures as our regular operating crew's experience level grows. Learning, and the layout owner's expectations, shouldn't cease at some arbitrary point.

But none of us do this for a living, at least not using 1950s-era work rules and procedures. So we look for prototypically based aids to make doing these "jobs" relatively easy to master and interesting to do, yet highly authentic in nature. Routing local cars by station number meets both criteria.

And there are certain limits to consider. Thinking that "We know this, so let's try this" could become a form of piling on. We could become so focused on learning the new stuff

that we forget the old stuff. Airline pilots do their jobs almost every day, yet they have to take refresher rides in realistic simulators at regular intervals to be sure some of the old stuff hasn't slipped away.

My sense is that we're now at a good level with our timetable and train-order operations and the realistic-format waybills, which I described in separate chapters in the second edition of my Kalmbach book, *Realistic Model Railroad Operations*. Adding even more complexity—"detail"—is probably going to detract rather than enhance the operating experience for most crew members.

Phil Monat (left) assumes his usual post as the westbound yardmaster at Frankfort, Ind. This is one of the most important jobs on my railroad, as it feeds the modeled Third Subdivision of the St. Louis Division. Delays here affect the performance of the entire railroad. But he has to balance adherence to timetable schedules with matching tonnage to locomotive capabilities, locomotive and crew availability, the superiority of oncoming eastbound trains, and other factors beyond the numbers printed in the timetable schedule.

3

The Frankfort yardmaster blocks local No. 45 by arranging the cars and waybills in station (ascending numerical) order (above). (Waybills are not normally leaned on cars!) The local crew can then refer to a track schematic at each town (see 2-6). Each track has a corresponding bill box (left). So when a loaded car is set out, its waybill is dropped into its bill box. Between sessions, I cycle its waybill to show it as an empty car for pick up.

4

1

CHAPTER ELEVEN

Guidance from the professionals

We should be very happy that scale model railroading attracts not only us "civilians" who have no ties to full-size railroading but also professional railroaders, **1**. Without exception, the many meets and conventions I attend each year are graced by the presence of friends who earn or earned their living working on the railroad. They invariably go out of their way to share their hard-won knowledge with those of us who otherwise would make seemingly logical assumptions about how railroads work that also would turn out to come up well short of reality.

I've always believed that it's a two-way street, however. In the bad ol' days of the 1960s and '70s, and probably decades before and after that period, it wasn't wise to tell your railroader boss that you were a railfan or model railroader. But I think that in those days when railroads were going bankrupt—when Conrail was formed

Left: The men and women who earn their living as professional railroaders, including well-known modeler Jack Ozanich (at left with "operator" Bob Milhaupt), are often model railroaders as well. What we learn from them can be the difference between playing with trains and realistically operating scale model railroads. *Craig Wilson*

Below: Brand-new EMD GP18 590 takes a spin on the turntable at Rangeley River Junction, Maine, to gets its low nose headed in the desired direction on Jack Ozanich's Atlantic Great Eastern. Jack hosts diesel-era operating sessions in the summer months when large numbers of crew members are more difficult to round up, as diesel-powered trains can be longer, hence fewer in number. *Craig Wilson*

3 Former NKP engineer Don Daily guided much of the thinking behind the way my model railroad operates. I was honored to have him participate in an operating session. He has some waybills in his right hand and his clearance Form A and a Form 19 train order in his left, so he's serving as the conductor as this eastbound leaves Veedersburg, Ind. *Mike DelVecchio*

out of the bones of the once mighty Pennsylvania and New York Central and quite a few colorful Eastern railroads—the only highly motivated, educated, and skilled candidates likely to apply for railroad jobs were fans and modelers. I know of several fellow Purdue Railroad Club members who became career railroaders only because they really liked railroading. The railroads were lucky to get them.

And we're also lucky to "get" them in the sense that they choose to participate in our hobby. They're the ones who patiently explain, time and time again, how a railroad and railroaders go about earning a living.

Railroading seems to be a simple enough system, what with two rails and flanged wheels to ensure cargo and passengers get from A to Z in the desired manner. But how that is actually accomplished is never quite what it seems. If we modelers are good at anything, it is at jumping to conclusions about how a railroad operates. Or, worse, we just don't bother to seek out "professional advice" and create our own methods and procedures that almost always miss out on some of the more interesting aspects of the workings of our rail transportation system. Exhibit A is the myriad waybill systems we create to forward freight cars when the prototype has a very workable system all ready for us to plagiarize, if in somewhat simplified form, as I discussed in Chapter 10.

But we're getting better at learning the ropes and applying our knowledge to modeling. Thanks to the support of model manufacturers and importers,

it is now easier than ever to model a specific prototype, even a small regional or shortline railroad. And once we progress past properly detailed locomotives and cars, and creating a context for our trains to run in, we increasingly listen to those who take their hobby time to explain to us how the equipment was used to move freight and passengers throughout the rail network.

As I was gathering photos for this book, I talked to Craig Wilson, one of the most gifted model railroad photographers I have ever worked with. Craig took the lead photo for this chapter and is in fact the "official

company photographer" for Jack Ozanich's proto-freelanced Atlantic Great Eastern. Craig was working on photos addressing different aspects of prototype-based freelancing on the AGE, thus helping me make the point that when done as well as Jack (a retired professional railroader) does it, it is a form of prototype modeling.

"As I look at these photos," Craig mused, "I am struck by something: Freelancing gives one the opportunity to do things that strike a particular interest. But the 'proto' aspect means that one can't just justify anything and everything. When Jack and I discuss adding new locomotives, freight cars, or paint schemes to the 'AGE world,' I find myself thinking about prototype railroading as much and maybe more than I would when modeling a specific prototype. These things have to fit into the real world of railroading circa 1959-1964.

"For example, Jack has a real fondness for six-axle EMD power (SD7s and SD9s), but the New England roads of that era didn't use them, so neither does the AGE, **2**. It is this attention to detail that makes everything just work."

There are also some highly knowledgeable modelers who have never worked for a railroad. I had to stay up pretty late to come up with a question that stumped the late Andy Sperandeo. But even they will quickly tell you that they learned a lot by talking to professional railroaders, or by reading what they took time to write. Former Western Pacific dispatcher Peter Josserand's *Rights of Trains* (still available as a softcover from Simmons-Boardman) has taught countless model railroaders the basics of train dispatching systems such as timetable and train-order (TTTO) and Centralized Traffic Control (CTC). I recommend it to anyone interested in realistic operation.

But I suspect that you could read that textbook 10 times without forming a clear picture of how a railroad operates. For that, you need to talk to someone who worked on the railroad, or a fellow modeler who has done that homework for you.

My good friend Steve King is a great example. In his younger days, Steve was a dispatcher on the Baltimore & Ohio using both TTTO and CTC dispatching systems. Steve is a natural teacher, and he holds classes for eager-beaver model railroaders who want to learn how to use such systems properly. Many of his students now have realistically operating railroads of their own, and they can then pass along what Steve taught them.

Steve and professional railroader Dave Sprau wrote *19 East, Copy Three* for the Operations Special Interest Group (opsig.org). They list it as out of stock, but copies may show up on eBay and at NMRA and Railroad Prototype Modelers conferences and swap meets.

It pays to seek out the professionals. They're around, probably as near as your local model railroad club, National Model Railroad Association division, or National Railway Historical Society chapter. Engage them in a discussion about aspects of railroading that are not yet clear to you. Encourage them to give talks so others can learn. Invite them to your operating sessions.

And, most of all, shake their hands as you thank them for helping us amateurs to understand this fascinating business of prototype railroading.

But do it now. Most of the steam-era railroaders are gone. The man I call the godfather of the Third Subdivision, Don Daily, **3**, is no longer with us. Don was a constant source of information and coaching about what to do and what was probably not a good idea. Don was the last man to learn to fire a steam locomotive out of the Frankfort, Ind., engine terminal, and he continued his career well into the post-merger years.

I can't recall the number of times I'd say that the NKP did such-and-so, only to hear Don reply, "No, you see…" I had overlooked a union work agreement or federal law that precluded what to me sounded like the way to do something. If I wanted to re-create the way the Nickel Plate operated out of Frankfort in the mid 1950s, I had to listen carefully to Don.

Try to find your Don while there's still time.

1

CHAPTER TWELVE
Lineside details

A 2-10-2 lopes across the mid-American prairie trailing a string of empty gondolas on Frank Hodina's proto-freelanced Chicago & Illinois Western, which has obvious ties to the Chicago & Illinois Midland. Note the leaning telephone poles, a reflection of gravity at work. *Frank Hodina*

One of the nicer outcomes of the trend toward prototype-based modeling is that we're all learning more about how things were done. Along the way, we're also developing more practical and realistic ways to model everyday "hardware." Take the fence lines and telegraph poles that often line the right-of-way, **1**, for example. Do we make them too tall—I certainly did, **2**—or fail to account for the effects of Mother Nature or how railroad "slide-rule" engineers account for same, as Frank Hodina (one of those engineers) did on his proto-freelanced Chicago & Illinois Western?

Many of us grew up in the era when we got, or wished we got, a train set for Christmas. Layout One was probably a racetrack oval on the living room floor. Layout Two wasn't much more sophisticated: an oval of sectional track on a 4x8-foot sheet of plywood supported by sawhorses.

The good ol' 4x8 is still a popular avenue into the hobby of model railroading, but it has some substantial drawbacks. It eats up a lot of floor space for starters, especially when you realize that three or possibly all four sides of the resulting layout have to be set away from the room walls to allow access to all parts of the platform.

So we've learned to cut the plywood into 8-foot lengths that are 24", 16", 12", or even 8" wide and to erect them as shelves along one, two, three, or all four sides of the railroad room. Supporting them on commercial bookcases makes the job go quickly.

It's not long before we realize that we've just saved ourselves a lot of work, time, and cost. Those narrow shelves don't eat up ground-covering materials like the deep scenes that a tabletop layout required. The lack of scenic depth is easily offset with photo backdrops, available from several suppliers as well as from your own camera and printer.

This approach reduces the task of building even a medium- to large-size home layout to a practical project. Rather than modeling sweeping vistas of mountain ranges or agricultural fields, we can model only the 100 feet or so between the fences that line the right-of-way. That translates to 7½" in N, 14" in HO, and about 24" in O. Cutting that 4x8 sheet into strips is already paying dividends!

But with such a narrow strip of land to scenic, we need to understand what we'd expect to find there. Often, fences lined the right-of-way. In the era when telegraph and telephone communications were the norm, there were pole lines along one side of the railroad. And don't forget the drainage ditches that lined both sides of the roadbed, **3**.

One scenic bugaboo we have to contend with when modeling on

2

My initial efforts at placing telegraph and telephone poles along the right-of-way resulted in some more closely resembling those found along an interurban. I have since shortened them so that the crossarms are at about the height of a locomotive cab.

narrow shelves is shadows. The more of the scene that we can include in the photo backdrop, the better. Frank Hodina, one of the master modelers who creates the patterns for resin models (resincarworks.com), avoided some shadows by gluing his fence (made from fabric) to the backdrop.

Frank has a degree in railroad engineering, so he tends to notice and model things the rest of us typically overlook. Note, for example, the leaning telegraph poles in the lead photo. It's not that he's a sloppy modeler, but I'll let Frank explain:

"Prototype poles might have been driven in straight, but over time they tend to lean in the direction perpendicular to the slope. There's a small cut here, so I leaned the poles toward the track. And once a pole starts leaning, the weight of the wires tends to pull the pole over more. It's why retaining walls have tie-backs into the soil: to keep them from tipping over."

Note, too, that the poles cast no shadows on the backdrop. That's not Photoshop; that's Frank.

Another lesson from this photo: Simple is good. Very good. Since we're invariably short of space, we tend

to cram everything we feel we need into the space we have rather than judiciously editing out everything but the essentials.

Frank is modeling the flatlands of Illinois with nary a major hill, let alone a mountain range, to break the monotony. But that very monotony can be spelled "realism." His railroad looks like it should, and it shouldn't look like the mountain-climbing Rio Grande.

That's an important lesson from basing even a freelanced railroad more closely on a prototype: It may not be spectacular, but it will look the part.

Modeling from memories

I guess all of our modeling is "from memories" in one way or another. Some are actual memories, be they from long ago or yesterday; others are memories we wish we had but were denied because it happened long ago or out of our reach. And many of those memories lead us to implant lineside details that we'd otherwise tend to overlook.

My entire circa-1954 model railroad is a memory of sorts. Some of those memories are from first-hand experiences in or near Cayuga, Ind., my 1950s hometown. The sprawling

Drainage ditches are an important lineside detail. I made them by raising the main line ½" on two layers of ¼" Homabed roadbed and the adjacent fields using ⅜" foam insulation panels. The ditch contours were achieved using fine sand and a roadbed cross-section template drawn along the track.

3

Frankfort, Ind., yard is backdated from personal visits in the 1960s. Other sections of the railroad are based on research conducted in more recent times, but I still rely on my memory, hit and miss though it is, to fill in between the lines of documented history.

I once wrote a Trains of Thought commentary about a trip that Jim Boyd, Steve King, Allen McClelland, and I made to the Virginias to gather information for our Appalachian coal haulers. We were in Bluefield, W.Va., and walking along the high retaining wall that borders the south side of what was then the Norfolk & Western's yard and engine terminal.

Jim, Steve, and I edged along the top of the wall, not noticing a big dog chained to his doghouse

behind an Exxon station. By the time Allen started across the narrow space between said dog and the wall, Blitzkrieg woke up with a start. Allen froze, and ol' Blitzy just stared at him. Allen then started edging slowly toward the now-fascinated rest of us, and the dog started edging toward Allen. The edging became a quick step and soon segued into an all-out footrace.

The chain saved the day as—whang!—the dog's journey came to an abrupt halt just short of Allen's netherlands. I modeled this scene on the Allegheny Midland at the moment when Allen and the dog both realized they had a mutual problem to resolve.

I confess that I believe that humorous scenes on model railroads, like humorous names given to model

railroads (yes, John Allen really did admit that he tired of the "gory and defeated" moniker), can quickly wear out their welcome, but one based on an actual event seemed appropriate.

Several of the usual suspects recently reminisced about life in the good ol' days, sharing tales and even photos of the Way Things Were. What's now a vacant parking lot in Wilkes-Barre, Pa., for example, was once a teeming railroad yard with a brick depot and freight house. It's hard to imagine that much steel, bricks, and mortar could be so utterly gone.

Walt Kierzkowski shared color photos of the colorful American Auto department store in downtown Scranton, just down the street from today's Steamtown. At Christmas time, the windows of such stores were filled with Lionel trains racing around ovals of three-rail track. It was Jean Shepherd's *A Christmas Story* coming to life. Like Jean, I lived in the Midwest back then and don't share any of the specific memories of the Northeast-bred group, but I could easily relate to them.

Wayne Sittner, whose modeling has graced the pages of the modeling periodicals from time to time, brought us back to railroading in miniature by sharing the accompanying photo of a scene from his childhood:

"In 1956, I spotted a Roll-Fast bike in the Kingston, Pa., American Auto store, and that bike became my Christmas present that year. I still have the bike, and it was such a part of my adolescence that I just had to model it to go with one of my portrait figures, which started as a Preiser model. In the scene, **4**, I'm looking for bottles to return for the 2-cent refund."

Wayne is a retired art teacher, and his considerable skill with a brush is complemented with another needed attribute: the power of observation. His modeling goes far beyond that needed to model a specific place and time. He invariably takes the viewer on a colorful trip to the past while at the same time triggering one's own personal memories related to scenes Wayne has modeled, as here.

The late John Coots, creator of the

Scale Structures Ltd. line of detailed structure kits and myriad detail parts to complement them, was a strong advocate of scale model railroading as an art form. Those who followed his lead—George Sellios of Fine Scale Miniatures and Art Fahie of Bar Mills Models come to mind—surely saw the art potential in their line of structures.

Often it's the little things that make all the difference. They help us tell a story and thereby convey a sense of time and place that far transcends merely good modeling. A kid with his bike looking for bottles to earn enough money to buy an ice-cold Coke on a hot summer day is the perfect example of a plausible lineside detail that adds life to a model railroad.

Caboose "motels"

Although a caboose track is not exactly "lineside" in that it's actually within a railroad yard, it is one of those often-overlooked details at the periphery of our yards that can add realism, operation, and a lot of interesting detail. And as we'll discuss in a moment, the caboose also served as a bed-and-breakfast for crews away from home terminals.

Back in the good ol' days, which many retired railroaders will tell you weren't really that great after all, each caboose was assigned to a specific conductor. I spent many an interesting afternoon on Nickel Plate Road wood caboose 1149 as it—and NKP conductor Bill Love, to whom it was assigned—overnighted in Michigan City, Ind. Bill had rigged a TV antenna to a power pole, and the engine crew took care to spot his caboose within hookup distance of that pole.

The caboose was literally his home away from home. When Bill was not at his home terminal in Peru, Ind., 1149 served as his motel. Most conductors were understandably fussy about how the rest of the rear-end crew treated their "home."

Clark Propst, who models the Minneapolis & St. Louis, wasn't sure where the local's crew that stayed overnight in Mason City, Iowa (River

4

Wayne Sittner takes his modeling to a higher level by modeling specific figures from his past—here himself as he parked his Christmas-gift bike long enough to look for soft-drink bottles to turn in for the deposit money. *Wayne Sittner*

5

When a retired Minneapolis & St. Louis employee visited Clark Propst's HO model of the Louie's yard at Mason City, Iowa, he recognized the place because of Clark's accurate modeling and confirmed the spot where they left their caboose overnight. *Clark Propst*

City of "Music Man" fame), spotted their caboose. When Clark invited a retired M&StL brakeman to see his railroad and asked him about that, the pro recognized the location because Clark had modeled it accurately and pointed to the exact spot, **5**. An old photo later confirmed this.

That was a win for Clark on several fronts. First, it is always rewarding to have a knowledgeable observer view

one's work, recognize the surroundings, and pronounce them authentic. It confirms that one has done his or her due diligence and produced an accurate rendition of a given time and place. And it confirms that one's operating scheme is correct: That caboose should indeed be spotted right there to allow the crew to get a good night's rest away from home.

CHAPTER THIRTEEN

Modeling grades

Thanks mainly to using metal wheels in all freight-car trucks, my 700-series Nickel Plate Berkshires of various brands can now haul decent-size trains up the serpentine climb out of the Wabash River Valley west of Cayuga, Ind. The grade is less than 2 percent, but that's a test for anything other than a heavily weighted brass engine.

Very few, if any, prototype railroads were ever built on a flat surface. That's good and bad—good in that modeling a surface that looks like a pool table isn't very interesting, and bad because it can be challenging to create the ups and downs that add visual and operational interest to our railroads in miniature. Model locomotives such as massive articulateds that look like mountain goats may not turn out to be as powerful as they appear. And smaller engines, especially some of the early brass lightweights, may balk at the slightest challenge.

A grade—slope, hill, incline, gradient—is measured as a percentage. So a grade that goes up 1 unit (be it a foot, a meter, or a mile) for every 100 units is a 1 percent grade; 5 units in 100 feet would be a 5 percent gradient. Our friends in the United Kingdom and Australia more typically measure grades ("banks," and helpers are "bankers") as a ratio. So a grade of 2 percent would shown as 1 in 50.

Grades are very important to modelers, not only because the full-size railroads that we're emulating have them but also because they help us achieve visual variety, create operating challenges, climb mountains, and allow us to raise one track over another to extend a run or to go between decks.

But they come with a price. A model locomotive that performs flawlessly and pulls a respectably long train on the level may fall on its face as it hits a significant grade. One that goes uphill like a champ may develop a bad case of the surges on its way down that same grade as slack in its gear train runs in and out. And simply building a smooth grade free of little "wows" that cause engines to stall or slip is harder than it looks, as is constructing smooth vertical curves at the base and top of a grade.

If ever there is a time to do a lot of test-running, it's before committing a track plan to three-dimensional form. That's when you need to check grades, especially those on curves, which add even more drag to a train. In fact, on full-size railroads, curves on grades are often "compensated"—that is, the grade is reduced as the degree of curvature increases (radius decreases)—to allow for the extra friction.

Today's modeler has discovered that it's easier than ever before to model a specific prototype to a high degree of accuracy, thanks to a wealth of products that depict the cars and locomotives of specific railroads. The prototype is our benchmark; match its major attributes and we're home free.

Well, maybe. And especially maybe with curves. Andrew Dodge and I were chatting about the grades on his former On3 Denver, South Park & Pacific and a predecessor HO railroad, and he confided that modeling the grades exactly like those on the prototype didn't work as well as he had expected. "Maybe it's because our railroads are built in such confined spaces and hence viewed up close. But whatever the reason, I found that duplicating, say, a

2

This light 2-8-2 on No. 45, the KC Local, is cresting Cayuga Hill with a rider car for Railway Express Agency shipments, a dozen cars, and a caboose at Humrick, Ill. The NKP's 2-8-4s slipped here so often that then-rookie fireman Don Daily said the ride was so rough from rail burns that he thought they had derailed.

4 percent grade wound up looking much too steep on my model thereof."

I ran into a different problem with an important grade on my HO edition of the Nickel Plate Road's St. Louis line. In the 1950s, I lived in Cayuga, Ind., at the foot of notorious Cayuga Hill, where the NKP had to climb out of the Wabash River Valley on its westward trek to the Mississippi. Berkshires that almost blew me over as they raced toward the hill were soon down on their knees, and often I could walk alongside the caboose. On occasion, a loud "Chow!" emanated from the air-brake system when the engineer dumped the air, cut the train in half, and "doubled the hill" to the summit just across the Illinois state line. This I absolutely had to model faithfully!

The grade was "only" 1.29 percent, but that told only half the story. A lot of reverse curves had been built into The Hill to slow descending trains by friction in the pre-air-brake era.

Gravity and friction aren't choosey; they'll stick it to an up-bound train just as forcefully.

No matter; all I had to do was to model the grade.

But was the goal to model the gradient to two decimal points or to cause trains to occasionally stall on the hill? I soon found that most of my model Berkshires pulling the 30-car trains the layout had been designed to accommodate, or even 20-car trains, wouldn't make that hill. In fact, some brands of Berkshires stalled with 12-car trains on the slightest grade!

What to do? Well, panic, for starters! But I started chipping away at the problem. I discovered that Bill Darnaby had encountered the same problem with his brass 4-8-2s and had resolved the problem to a great extent by equipping the freight cars with Accurail sideframes and InterMountain metal wheelsets.

Next, I moved the summit another 20 feet to the west, thus reducing

the grade, and added weight to locomotives where possible. I also tested one of Dennis Realley's 2-8-4s that had some drivers coated with Bullfrog Snot—a liquid "traction tire" that can be applied to any locomotive—with promising results.

Who would have guessed a little ol' 1.29 percent grade would cause such grief? Had I done more testing, I

Midland Road 2-6-6-2 Mallet 928 (above) is typical of the steam power that handled coal shifters in the central Appalachians owing to both steep grades and sharp curves in the "hollers." This locomotive, a Pacific Fast Mail import rebuilt by Cheat River Engineering, is on display at the National Model Railroad Association's scale model railroading exhibit at the California State Railroad Museum in Sacramento, Calif. It posed with an AM hopper car and caboose on my NKP (right) before heading west.

3

would have.

Back in the Allegheny Midland days, I had used 30" mainline curves and 2.5 percent grades. This was before today's high-quality plastic Berkshires were available, so most of the fleet were Key brass imports. Cheat River Engineering had filled the boilers with weight, so those heavy 2-8-4s could take 25-car trains up Cheat River

Grade without breaking a sweat.

But one had to be careful about loaded coal trains descending those grades, as some diesel-powered trains would surge as slack in the gear boxes ran in and out, and the head-end power could actually slide through a switch at the bottom of the grade if the engineer didn't have his train under control.

Today's locomotive drives are much better than much of what came from the factory in the 1970s and '80s, so the main challenge is to determine what your favorite locomotives, especially steam locomotives, will pull up your planned grades and around your planned minimum radius curves.

And, as Andrew Dodge discovered, how will they look while doing that?

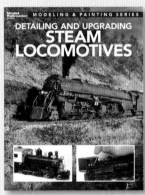
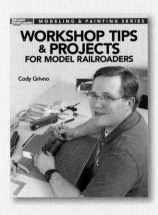
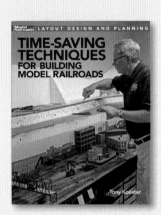